St. Augustine Pirates and Privateers

Theodore Corbett

THE
History
PRESS

Published by The History Press
Charleston, SC 29403
www.historypress.net

Copyright © 2012 by Theodore Corbett
All rights reserved

First published 2012

Manufactured in the United States

ISBN 978.1.60949.721.7

Library of Congress CIP data applied for.

Contents

Acknowledgements

This book represents an earlier dream that was not completed. I began research on St. Augustine in the 1970s with the help of a Del Amo Fellowship to Spain and visits to the St. Augustine Historical Society's library, where the staff, especially Jacqueline Bearden, was most helpful. While the articles and papers found in the bibliography were published, I was never able to put together a book on the city of St. Augustine. When retirement freed me to pursue projects, I decided to focus on the popular topic of pirates and privateers. Susan R. Parker, executive director of the St. Augustine Historical Society, recently looked over the manuscript and wrote, "It is good that there will be a publication that gathers all of this material."

I dedicate this book to the memory of my father, Theodore G. Corbett, who read *Treasure Island* to me when I was a boy.

Guide to Vessels

GALLEONS

While galleons were the standard fighting ships of the Atlantic, they also carried cargo, especially if it was bullion, which was a matter of state. The galleon had at least two decks from stem to stern, with its main batteries in broadside and castles on the main deck, fore and aft, although these would be reduced and streamlined by the eighteenth century. Generally, galleons carried at least forty guns, and later ships-of-the-line carried up to ninety guns, requiring three decks.

ARMED MERCHANT SHIPS

Merchant ships like carracks supported galleons and were often of larger tonnage for cargo but usually had less firepower, a greater concern being speed. They could carry the highest caliber guns, and some even had three decks, so that on their own they were fit enough to ward off pirates.

Pinnaces and sloops were smaller craft that were decked, had one or more masts, sat low in the water and were faster and handier than the larger craft. They were meant for reconnaissance and dispatch services and were capable of shore work. They carried no more than a dozen guns. Merchant ships, as well as galleons and ships-of-the-line, carried or towed launches or barges for use in harbors and coastal waters.

Frigates

In the seventeenth century, the term was used for ships too small to stand in the line of battle but capable of patrolling. A group of them were a formidable adversary. Spanish frigates were similar to sloops, built for speed, with no more than a dozen guns. By the eighteenth century, however, frigates had evolved into a ship square-rigged on all three masts and were as long as a ship-of-the-line, but they were faster and with twenty-eight or more guns used for patrolling coastal waters and escorting merchant ships or privateers.

Oared Craft

Galliots were small oared craft popular in America; they often had a sail.

Xebecs were Spanish hybrids. While they carried oars, they had Lateen riggings for speed and were large enough to carry cargo.

Barcos luengos were large oared craft that could carry a hundred men.

Piroques (periaguas) were dugout canoes, usually made from a cypress log. Larger ones had a sail. The Timucuan Indians introduced them to the Spanish, and they were used in the British colonies along their coasts.

Introduction

The image of piracy most know by the general public, especially those who watch Errol Flynn, Tyrone Power or Johnny Depp movies, is not what you will find here. Piracy is defined as "the...indiscriminate taking of property or persons with violence, on or by descent from the sea [and] involves the traditional rights of members of communities to appropriate to themselves the property of others." Thus, it has to do with robbery, destruction, savagery and cruelty, the essential ingredients of what we would call crime. But there is more to piracy than this.

Romance aside, most pirates had once been privateers, and most privateers were affiliated with the legitimate rise of navies and states, supported locally by governors and officials. Sea-going merchants also played a role in developing privateers, but in their case, service to the state had to be profitable, so that conflict of interest was a given. Pirates and privateers could not exist without each other. It is often impossible to differentiate them. Pirates were definitely fewer in number since they tried to pass for privateers to avoid the hangman. Ultimately, piracy cannot be separated from privateering: the one is dependent on the other.

Leaders of European nation-states felt that privateers represented a covert form of war. Even France, despite the lack of a naval tradition like England or Spain, would come to need privateers. In 1695, Sebastian Vauban, the great French designer of fortifications, wrote a memorandum urging Louis XIV not to strengthen his land army or battle fleets but to defeat his enemies by taking up privateering. He contended it was the English and Dutch who were France's main enemies and that their strong navies and financial subsidies to other states made them formidable. Their wealth, moreover, came from trade, which allowed them to be "the masters and dispensers of the most solid money in Europe." Privateering warfare was the best way of combating this, for it struck at the economic sinews of war. He predicted that the English and Dutch would ruin themselves in trying to protect themselves from privateers. He contended that until now, privateering in France had depended upon the unaided efforts of private individuals, who had limited resources and took all the risks. Instead of encouraging them, the state had offered legal vexations, adjudication of the vessels taken as prizes and heavy duties so that many a shipowner could not afford to participate. Thus, Vauban argued, privateers should be granted all manner of privileges, and he concluded that privateering would "enrich the state, train many good officers for the king and force his enemies to sue for peace on more reasonable conditions." Here was a plea for state-sponsored privateering.

This book approaches pirates from a military perspective, which conceives of them as Vauban did—as auxiliaries and irregulars that supported state navies. This is not the usual perspective because the developing navies were often charged with rooting out piracy. Piracy was a form of war and at the same time commerce based on profit taking. While states could promote it, decisions on how to use it were made locally.

The states of Spain, France and England set up highly regulated systems of trade from the perspective of the mother country, but their local representatives, the governors of colonies and captains of the rising navies, acted as the immediate regulator of pirates and privateers. The rules were continually bent. At times they encouraged privateers or looked the other way with pirate activities. However, they also hunted the pirates down and hanged them. They came to feel that one of the best ways of subduing pirates or naval enemies was to enlist other pirates against them.

Pirates and privateers were maritime predators who operated opportunistically from state-sanctioned privateering to lawless piracy. Plundering was not limited to pirates; it was the right of sailors and soldiers on privateers.

All freebooters relied on access to ports if they were to survive in an increasingly hostile political environment. Merchants, as well as colonists along the Atlantic coast, profited from their connections to marauders. It was only possible for navies to successfully suppress piracy after the 1720s, when the colonial authorities managed to close their ports to pirates.

Far from being revolutionaries, pirates always sought the king's pardon as loyal subjects. In 1721, on the pirate ships *Morning Star* and *Good Fortune*, the crews gathered and drafted a letter most democratically so that none would be singled out as a ringleader of the group. It was sent to George I of Britain on a ship from Jamaica. It reads:

> *That we your Majesty's most loyal subjects have at sundry times...been forced* [by their Captain Bartholomew Roberts] *to enter into and serve...as pirates, much contrary to our wills and inclinations: And we your loyal subjects* [left Roberts] *and ran away with aforesaid* [ships] *with no other intent...than the hopes of obtaining your Majesty's most gracious pardon. And that we your Majesty's most loyal subjects may with more safety return to our native country and serve the Nation unto which we belong...without fear of being prosecuted by the injured, whose estates have suffered by the said Roberts...during our forcible detainment.*

The crew and ships then retired to an island near the coast of Cuba and were idle, awaiting news of their petition, which was never answered. Later, some of the crew were caught and hanged, but a number did finally reach England, where they melted into the population.

PRIVATEERS

What technically separated privateers from pirates was that privateers held state authorization or a letter of marque that justified their conduct in the service of the state. During the early 1500s in Spain, the Catholic king, in order to prevent robbery of Spanish ships and to upset enemies' trade, issued letters of marque to experienced seamen, most of whom inhabited villages along the Spanish coast. The crown would protect the privateers on the condition that they harass the enemy ships.

An example of a late seventeenth-century Spanish letter of marque is that of the frigate *Nuestra Señora del Rosario*, built in the San Sebastian area of Cantabria. It announces:

> *By virtue of the present document, the said captain, Pedro de Ezábal, can start privateering with the said frigate against people of war, to acquire the necessary arms and ammunition, and sail along the coasts of Spain, Barbary and France, fighting and capturing any ships of French nationality they find, due to the war declared with that Crown; any other Turkish and Arab corsairs they can find; and any other ships belonging to enemies of*

my Royal Crown, under the condition and declaration that they cannot, under any circumstances, go to nor pass the coasts of Brazil, the Terceira, Madeira and Canary islands, nor the coasts of the Indies.

Note that the privateer's activities were limited to the coasts of Spain, the Barbary and France but that they were not to move toward or go to the Americas. Spanish authorities insisted upon a certain control over their privateers.

The privateers were required to give the captured goods to these authorities, usually a justice or governor of the nearest province, for distribution. However, certain privateers divided the take without waiting for a royal bull, and others continued to operate when the letter of marque was out of date, even in times of peace between Spain and its enemies. Spain called privateers, "corsairs," a term Anglos associate with outright piracy and, no doubt, some corsairs became pirates.

The process of acquiring and maintaining a Spanish letter of marque, was very similar to that of England, except that instead of a certificate from a local customs collector, the privateer captain had to swear before a notary that he agreed to government regulations on conspiring. In addition, the Spanish government had the right to tax the proceeds from the sale of a prize.

THE CREW

In terms of manning ships, navies, merchants, privateers and pirates vied for scarce sailors and soldiers. Privateers had an edge in this competition because their pay was higher, the food was plentiful and the work shifts shorter. Merchant ships had the smallest possible crew because cargo space was the highest priority and speed in transporting the cargo the next. Privateer and pirate crews were usually large, requiring men to board another ship, to maneuver on land against a port, to conduct a siege if necessary and to sail the captured prizes (ships). Broadsides of cannon fire, so crucial to victory in naval warfare, may have been used to corner pirates, but hand-to-hand fighting at close quarters was what the Royal Navy had to adopt to kill Edward Teach, the notorious Blackbeard.

Most men who went to sea came from or lived near a port that was almost a city-state, often established on a coastal or river domicile. If strategic, these ports were embellished by a political authority with fortifications, docks,

Capture of the Pirate Blackbeard by Jean Leon Gerome Ferris, 1718. *Courtesy of Wikimedia Commons.*

quays, light houses and shipbuilding facilities. Favored locations for pirates and privateers were ports with few trade restrictions and no customs duties, where a degree of free trade flourished. Diversity of origin, race and religion in such ports was also welcomed, as it broke down social barriers, even attracting Jews. Sailors joined artillerymen and soldiers on vessels outfitted at these ports.

The crews of privateers and pirates were from an underclass created by unfavorable economic conditions. Landlubbers and soldiers were not lacking on pirate ships, but they played a secondary role when sailing. Most sailors had originally been pressed or sentenced to join a navy, especially the galleys, and observers made sport of the fact that they were the sweepings of the streets. The strict discipline and conditions of the navy made sailors want to serve on merchant ships or become pirates. A theory exists that pirates flourish in periods of peace at the end of wars because surplus sailors are unemployed and have to seek desperate alternatives. However, in peace or war, a shortage of sailors always existed. Moreover, pirates were immune to being in the labor market. They operated independently for only short

Above: Engraving showing Portuguese ships departing from Lisbon and the Lisbon quay with sailors, galleons and smaller vessels by Theodor de Bray, circa 1593. *Courtesy of Wikimedia Commons.*

Left: Engraving by Gaspar Bouttats depicting a scene from the novel *Guzmán de Alfarche* by Mateo Alemán. The picaro Guzman is being seized for his transgressions. In the novel, he is sentenced to life as a galley slave. *Courtesy of Wikimedia Commons.*

durations, one or two cruises at the most, and were constantly prepared to return to law-abiding society.

Crews came from the lower social classes, and only a minority knew how to write. Sailors had specialties; in Spain, Basque-speaking seamen were more experienced with the rigging and rope than they were at piloting. The Basques and Catalans had their own language, so that many did not understand Spanish, although the more experienced sailors did. Crews were ethnically mixed, Spanish ships having French, Flemish or Irish members, although it was not customary to have many of them. As the bottom of the social order in the Americas, blacks found service as a sailor or soldier to be rewarding. It offered them the opportunity to bear arms, the possibility of gaining a degree of freedom and even better pay. In America, free Spanish blacks were extremely loyal to Spanish authorities because they had freed them from slavery. Conversely, the fear of slave uprisings in British colonies was endemic, and the docks were strictly patrolled to stifle unrest.

The most important crew member of a large privateer ship was the captain, who played the role of middleman between the shipowners and investors and the crew members. If it was a pirate ship, he alone counteracted and guided the crew. The captain was the one who decided whether or not to go into combat and was in charge of discipline on board. Pirates ignored investors and sometimes even the captain when they distributed their shares of plunder. Pirates could depose a captain and maroon him to an open boat to forge for himself.

Next in rank was the lieutenant captain, who would substitute for the captain in case of his illness or death and would stand a round of guard. The master supervised the nautical steering and administered the provisions. The pilot directed navigation and gave orders to the helmsmen. The boatswain carried out the captain's orders and was in charge of the rigging and protection against fire. His assistant was the guardian, who was in charge of cleaning the ship, the smaller boats and supervising the boys.

A sailing crew was split into three categories: the seamen, the cabin boys and the boys. The first two groups looked after the sails and navigation, while the third was in charge of cleaning, managing food supply, acquiring strands for rope and leading prayers on board ship. In addition to these were the constable (who was in charge of the artillery, the artillerymen and the soldiers for boarding), the carpenter, the chaplain, the clerk and the surgeon. Two other jobs on pirate or privateer ships existed: that of officer in charge of prisoners, who would govern a captured ship until reaching port and selling it, and the supervisor, who controlled everything that took place during the voyage, the behavior of the crew and the avoidance of fraud. On merchant ships, this crew was considerably reduced.

When captured by the state navies and authorities, most crews tried to prove that they were privateers, not pirates. A French privateer, captained by Lewis Guittar, was captured by the English in 1700. While fighting against them, Guittar had first demanded a pardon but finally surrendered to the governor of Virginia who promised quarter, offering Guittar and his men His Majesty's mercy. The Virginia court examined the evidence and then transferred the accused to London, where despite their claims of innocence, Guittar and twenty-three of his crew were tried for piracy and, several months later, hanged.

In the Virginia court, Guittar's crew spoke of their experience on the ship, claiming they became pirates against their will. Four of the pirates, aged sixteen to twenty-two, from Picardy, Nantes and Saintonge, alleged they were forced to join the pirates. One sixteen-year-old stated that, having been shipwrecked, he and others survived and existed on a rock until Captain Guittar's ship rescued them. One crew member was identified as a prisoner and not a pirate, a distinction that put him under military law. Still, most were hanged.

Of course, merchants and investors were never pirates, but they gambled their money on privateers and could offer support to certain pirates. They traded with them, bought their booty and acted as a buffer for them when they were in port. They represented the commercial aspect of privateers and pirates. Merchants involved in profitable trade and those who wanted to contribute to war efforts sought letters of marque. Their activity was either casual, taking prizes as concerns secondary to the promotion of trade, or seriously dependent on the number and worth of prizes their privateers brought to admiralty courts.

Woodes Rogers, a Bristol merchant and eventually governor of the Bahamas, sought to support British expansion as the commander of a privateer fleet. He was often tempted to act like a pirate. But his investors kept control of him. In Bristol, on July 14, 1708, the owners and directors of this private venture formed a constitution for a voyage to America. They appointed three captains, including Woodes Rogers, and these three would make decisions in their council meetings. Attacks on the enemy were to be discussed in council, discontent was to be settled, offenders tried and all transactions registered in a book by the clerk. It became necessary to hold frequent councils, as the owners wanted lists of men and plunder. After sailing, the council outlined how plunder and prizes would be treated.

Every member of the crew got a share, but there was also punishment for hiding plunder. Disputes over plunder were to be handled by officers. Such restrictions were meant to maximize the investors' profit.

COASTAL WATERS

Pirate activity could be focused on the high seas, but it was the coast that was the pirates' favored environment. Raids by privateers and pirates combined land and sea operations, in which the community below the fortifications or the surrounding countryside was most likely to be sacked. This meant that smaller oared craft that could penetrate harbors and rivers were the vessel of pirate activity.

In the island-studded Caribbean, the pirate ship of choice was not a ship-of-the-line or heavily armed merchant vessel; instead, it might be a sloop or even an oared galley with a sail, built for war rather than trade. In sixteenth-century Europe, galleys were the only ships built strictly for a military purpose, having little room for cargo. They were long and narrow with a shallow draw. A 180-foot galley had only a 19-foot beam and a depth of a mere 7.5 feet, superb for maneuvering in the shallows. They were best suited for the Mediterranean where, propelled by oars of as many as 300 condemned prisoners, the galleys could reach high speeds. The rowers were treated like slaves, chained to their benches where they rowed, ate and slept. Usually there was a bow canon with four smaller artillery pieces and fourteen anti-personal weapons.

In the late 1500s, galleys had given way to galleons on trade routes, especially in the Atlantic. A galleon not only could carry more cargo, but it could remain out of range of the galley's guns and keep them from coming close and boarding. However, in ports and along the coast where shallowness prevented the larger ships from functioning, the galleys could still maneuver and quickly surround an enemy vessel and destroy them by firepower, ramming or boarding. In 1631, when the Spanish governor of Cumana expelled the Dutch and pirates from Tortuga Island off the coast of Venezuela, he arrived in a galleon but used smaller oared craft to take the port. In 1690, a fleet of French galleys raided Teignmouth on the Devonshire coast, an area famous for the number of captains and sailors it has produced.

Later in America, Spaniards built sail galleys to patrol the Caribbean and North American coast against raiders and pirates. Most privateer and pirate

Plan of Tortuga Island and its Dutch settlements, circa 1628–31. The plan shows the landing of a Spanish assault force under Governor Benito Arias Montano of Cumana against the Dutch forts and pirates. While the galleon is firing a broadside, smaller oared galleys do most of the work. *Courtesy Archivo General de Indias.*

raiders used light sloops or Spanish frigates. But when pirates and privateers wanted to hide and refit, oared-type craft were still useful. Many a battle was decided by which ships could be refloated after being stuck on a sand bar at low tide. Thus, rowed craft of any kind continued to be valuable for warfare in America to the end of the eighteenth century.

Chapter One
St. Augustine, the Noble City

Privateering was a well-established part of Spain's commerce and defense when St. Augustine was founded in 1565. Located on Florida's eastern coastal waters, St. Augustine became a *presidio*, or military community, with a garrison of young single men and an annual subsidy of coin, food and goods to sustain the garrison. It was dependent upon a series of flimsy wooden forts for protection until 1671, when work was begun on Castillo de San Marcos, a stone bastioned fortification that visitors can still see today. The other aspect of its defense was the treacherous sand bar at the entrance to its harbor. Without a pilot, a ship was likely to founder and many friendly vessels anchored outside the harbor entrance and had their cargo ferried by launch to St. Augustine's docks. The city of St. Augustine sprawled below the Castillo to the south. While efforts were eventually made to fortify the community with a ditch, earthen wall and palisade, the population, when threatened, took refuge within the walls of the Castillo or its predecessors, and the undefended city and its suburbs were easily sacked.

St Augustine became a community dependent on outside influences for its prosperity and growth. Mortality was high; in the years 1727 and 1728 alone over 10 percent of the population died. Births per marriage were also low so that the chance of natural population increase was minimal. Decline in population was prevented, however, by the constant influx of male immigrants to serve in the garrison or government offices. Yet there were healthier times. From 1683 to 1702 and from 1753 to 1762, the number of births per marriage was high, while mortality in the second period declined

Castillo San Marcos, St. Pedro bastion, completed in 1695. *Courtesy of Wikimedia Commons.*

to the point that there no longer were epidemics. These two eras were the result of the influx of population from the construction of Castillo de San Marcos and, later, efforts to better defend the community and open it to trade and privateering with British colonies.

From 1658 to 1691, male immigration to St. Augustine moved from two directions, one wave westward from the Iberian Peninsula and a second wave northward from Mexico and Cuba. From 1692–1756, the movement from Spanish America was greatly diminished, while the movement of blacks from Cuba and the Carolinas supplemented the Iberian thrust. The typical migrant was a single male and had come from a large urban center, probably among the surplus landless population of Seville, Cadiz, Granada, Malaga, Cordoba, Mexico City, Puebla or Havana. Often a beggar for food in the mendicant tradition, he was swept from the streets by a press gang or taken from the prisons and

San Diego of Alcala Feeding the Poor or The Soup of the Foolish by Bartholomew Murillo, circa 1645. Begging was popular in all Spanish cities. This painting does not show able-bodied young men around the soup pot, indicating they preferred the navy. *Courtesy Royal Academy of San Fernando, Madrid.*

conscripted, ultimately contributing to the Castillo's construction or serving in garrison. Some of these immigrants found a livelihood as crews on privateers.

To offset the possibility of such rootless service, St. Augustine had a high marriage rate, so that single males were integrated into the community. Most of the brides and brides-to-be already lived in St. Augustine, as women were present from the city's earliest settlement, when marriages often involved Indians. Even if they were riffraff, the single men claimed the status of peninsulars or criollos, while the women represented greater racial diversity since many were of Native American or African descent. Most families chose to ignore miscegenation, claiming to be criollos. The concerns of family honor, property and the Catholic Church conspired to make these single men marry and become citizens of St. Augustine.

Painting depicting the mixed marriage of Captain Martin Garcia de Loyola to Beatriz Clara Coya, an Inca princess. Placed in the Church of the Society of Jesus in Cuzco, Peru, in the second half of the seventeenth century, it reflected the Jesuit support for similar marriages of whites and Indians. *Courtesy of Wikimedia Commons.*

This community would be the victim of pirate raids for twenty years in the late seventeenth century. In the eighteenth century, it would become much more of an adversary of privateers and pirates from the Bahamas and the Carolinas. By the 1720s and 1740s, it would be a privateer base seeking to confront the enemies of the Spanish Empire.

Chapter Two
Spain's Fleets and Navy

S t. Augustine was a backwater in terms of trade and wealth, yet its location gave it an important role in imperial rivalries, enhancing the need for privateer and pirate activities. As a presidio, St. Augustine would have the role of protecting Spanish shipping in the Florida Channel above the Bahamas. From the beginning, Spanish imperial policy was governed by the need to protect the ships that brought wealth from the West Indies to designated Spanish ports. Spain sought to overcome two threats: adverse weather and pirates. Traffic to the Indies began to be organized into convoys in 1543 when flotas (fleets) first incorporated warships to accompany and protect merchant vessels. The last leg of the return journey was from Havana to Spain, traveling by the site of St. Augustine. In 1564, the dispatch of such fleets was first recognized in the crown's ordinances, leading to St. Augustine's own establishment a year later. These fleets and designated convoys would ultimately become the basis of the Spanish navy and spawn privateers to cripple their enemies.

FLEETS AND ARMADAS

In the sixteenth century, Spanish authorities developed a most consistent way of combating pirates. They created organized convoys of merchantmen, which were protected by several naval galleons. Such a fleet was too strong for even the most audacious pirate fleet to challenge. Spanish authorities became proficient at organizing fleets. This is also seen in the creation of the

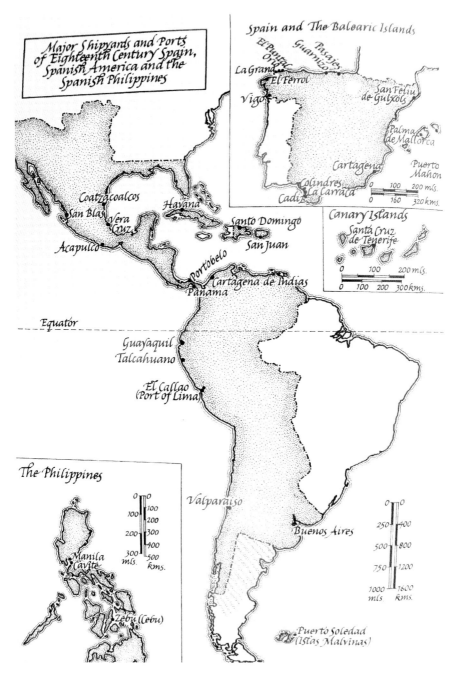

Shipyards and ports of eighteenth-century Spanish America, Spain and the Canary Islands.
Courtesy Naval Institute, Annapolis.

famous Armada against England in 1588, which baffled the English even in their own channel, because of its tight crescent ship formation that endured the continued English efforts to penetrate it and because it was broken only by the weather. At that time, armadas were made up of private ships that the crown either rented or asked to be built. In years when an armada was not needed, a Spanish navy scarcely existed. An armada had components from all over the multi-state Hapsburg Empire. The only possibility a pirate had against them was if an individual straggler was separated from the fleet before it was able to rejoin. Another opportunity for pirates was to work as a salvager when weather broke up a fleet, a circumstance that happened a few times along the eastern Florida coast.

The 1564 ordinances assumed the dispatch of two fleets from Seville, one heading for San Juan de Ulua on the Mexican coast, the other for Cartagena de Indies on the Colombian coast. From Cartagena, the fleet would sail to Portobello, where it would pick up merchants who had traveled there from Peru. Ships from ports outside this route had to sail to Spain with permits. At the time, the Spanish crown feared any ships traveling alone without a naval escort would be taken by pirates or engage in contraband activities.

Given the choice of confronting pirates or exposing the fleets to storms, the latter was considered more dangerous, so fleets were timed to sail when the weather was best. For fleets traveling to New Spain, April and May were favored for departure. They could arrive in time to avoid the storms that hit the Gulf of Mexico and Caribbean at the end of summer. The fleets to Cartagena and Panama left for Spain in July or August, so that they would arrive after the rainy season. The total round trip would take nine or ten months.

As noted, the return of both fleets always included a landfall at Havana. Its magnificent harbor was located at the point of winds and currents that led directly back to Spain. The return trip was longer and more dangerous than the outbound voyage. The fleet sailed north in the Florida Channel and then east toward the Azores and finally toward Cape of Saint Vicente, the farthest southwestern corner of the Iberian Peninsula. Both the Azores and the Cape swarmed with pirates, so that even though they were almost home, this could be the most dangerous portion of the voyage. While merchantmen carried most of the goods, the galleons came to carry the most precious cargo from the standpoint of the state: silver bars, gold and silver coins and jewels. With the arrival of each fleet, the Spanish crown could continue to survive and dominate the world of European politics.

The number of times the fleets failed to appear at Seville or Cadiz was minimal. Only one New Spain fleet was taken in 1628 at Matanzas, Cuba, by

Engraving of Matanzas Bay, Cuba, showing the capture of the New Spain fleet on September 28, 1628. *P. Conradi, 1787.*

the Dutch under Piet Heyn, a pirate who became a Dutch admiral. He had an impressive thirty-two-ship fleet and more than 3,500 men when he surprised the small fleet en route to Havana from New Spain. The flota consisted of only 11 merchantmen and two guarding galleons under command of veteran General Juan de Benavides. When the Dutch blocked Benavides's way to Havana, he and his officers decided to retreat to Matanzas port, unload the cargo and then meet the Dutch in combat. However, the Spanish fleet ran aground in the port's shallows. After vacillation, Benavides ordered his ships abandoned and burned to keep them from the enemy. All fifteen ships were lost, and the Dutch carried away booty estimated at 12 million florins. Benavides was charged with negligence by the Spanish crown, which needed an example, and despite his noble lineage, his throat was formally cut on a scaffold in 1634, the official death sentence for a noble. Regardless of the loss, the second fleet of the year, the Tierra Firme fleet, arrived in Spain. The crown's galleons continued to sail because they carried the silver and jewels, crucial to sustain the Spanish Empire's numerous commitments.

The Navy

The sixteen-century fleets and armadas did not really make a navy in the sense of forming a permanent naval body that was devoted to dominating the seas. The Spanish navy began to take shape from 1594 to 1620, the last years of Philip II's reign. At the time, the Spanish crown came to own or lease all the ships the state used and then created permanent fleets to continuously protect Spanish home waters, where the threat of pirates was acute. The expanded navy was financed by a permanent averias tax on both public and private trade of merchandise and treasure. A committee of the Casa de la Contratacíon at Seville administered the tax, and while it was chronically in arrears, it became an integral part of Spain's military planning. The galleons for the Indies fleets were now financed by this tax.

Next Philip III established control over shipbuilding to improve the quality of Spanish naval ships. While attempts were made to build the crown's own ships, contacting private shipyards was the best way of obtaining quality ships, and this led to the development of shipyards in Cantabria.

Philip III also unfolded a campaign against pirates, who were defined broadly as foreigners aimed at breaking the Spanish monopoly over Indies trade and the Spanish colonists who cooperated with them. The crown fostered privateering by letting Spanish colonists keep the goods they captured from pirates and illegal traders. Another decree to combat pirates ordered

Portrait of Phillip III, from the Ratification of the Treaty of London in 1604. *Courtesy of the Public Record Office, London.*

colonists to move inland away from temptation; it was not popular with colonists involved in smuggling. The governor of Cartagena put together a fleet that routed English and French pirates and took enemy ships and all their cargo.

By the time Philip IV ascended the throne in 1621, the navy had become a reality beyond the initial existence of the original three Iberian squadrons. Plans for a similar fleet in the New World were often broached, but Spain's commitments were so vast that resources could never be spared to establish a similar system of permanent squadrons. Without such squadrons, Spanish America became dependent on privateers.

PRIVATEERS

While Spanish privateers had long existed, Philip IV would formally license corsairs and privateers in order to protect Spanish shipping in Europe and America. The Decree of 1621 set down laws of privateering as General Laws, rules for carrying on these activities. The laws primarily affected the Spanish province of Guipuzcoa and its chief port San Sebastian, transforming it into the leading privateer area of the Basque Country, Cantabria. While San

View of the Bay of San Sebastian by Luis Paret y Alcázar, circa 1786. San Sebastian chose to become Cantabria's premier privateering port. *Courtesy Palacio de la Zarzuela, Patrimonio Nacional.*

Sebastian had lost out to rival Bilbao as a commercial port, so it sought to revitalize its trade through privateering. It had better facilities for building large ships than river-bound Bilbao. Between 1622 and 1697, there were forty-one licensed shipowners in San Sebastian and 271 privateering ships. Some shipowners were foreign, mostly Basque-French, Bretons and Irish. This expansion meant an increase in privateering from the traditional Basque coast and the Indies to the waters of northern Europe and France, England, the Netherlands and Ireland. Privateers from the San Sebastian area captured 120 ships, most of which were carrying merchandise from La Rochelle's Huguenot pirates and the Netherlands.

This situation led to confrontation between the owners of privateers and traders, who were hostile to privateering because they felt it frightened off other merchants. To the consternation of Bilbao's merchants, San Sebastian privateers would await prey in the vicinity of Bilbao's estuary. Outstanding was San Sebastian's Captain Agustín de Arizabalo, who situated himself at the mouth of Bilbao port in 1658, catching every merchant ship coming from the north of Europe, France, the Netherlands and Portugal. The San Sebastian privateers were accused of acting like pirates, entering into the Cantabrian ports as if they were the privateers' home ports to plunder foreigners with total disregard for legitimate trade.

THE NAVY TAKES ON CARIBBEAN PIRATES

As a result of the capture of the Indies fleet by the Dutch in 1628, Philip IV produced further reforms from 1629 to 1635. He determined that the Indies fleets could sail with only galleons—no merchants—so that before they reached their destinations, the flotas could take on wartime responsibilities like destroying pirate enclaves. Pirates gathered in the smaller isolated Caribbean islands (which Spain did not have the resources to settle) and combined their raiding with growing lucrative tobacco crops or smoking meat. These fringe islands had been occupied by French, Dutch and English refugees, often without formal government. Thus, Spanish fleets dubbed galiflotas were now prepared to root out pirates in their lairs before they could perform their depredations.

The first of the galiflotas left Cadiz in mid-August 1629, under command of Fadrique de Toledo, who was charged not only to carry the traditional treasure but to seek Dutch fleets and dislodge pirates and interlopers from the smaller islands of the Caribbean. The galiflota continued from the

Philip IV with a dwarf, by Gaspar de Crayer. *Courtesy of Wikimedia Commons.*

Canaries after confronting a Dutch fleet and taking seven ships. From there, the fleet moved on toward the island of Nevis, southeast of Puerto Rico, where an English colony exported tobacco and had forged a relationship with pirates who possessed ships and ammunition. Toledo surprised ten tobacco-laden ships in the harbor and took most of them. After losing twenty-two men, the English fled into the woods, abandoning the harbor and fort. A day later, they surrendered, and Toledo dismantled and burned the fort, tobacco warehouses and town.

With his prisoners, Toledo moved to San Cristóbal Island, another tobacco-growing pirate center of English and French settlers. The island was fortified in several places and had been warned of the galiflota's intentions. The Spaniards landed unopposed and captured the English fort after an artillery barrage. The English surrendered and the French forts followed them. After promising they would never return, the prisoners were sent back to Europe in captured Dutch vessels. In seventeen days, Toledo had captured 129 cannons, 42 mortars, 1,350 muskets and harquebuses and 3,000 prisoners.

The galiflota went on to Cartagena, where it wintered and returned in 1630 with an impressive amount of Indies treasure. The Spaniards needed this victory over the pirates to offset the previous loss of the flota to the Dutch. Philip IV was so pleased that he commissioned artist Félix Castelo to do a painting commemorating Fadrique's recapture of San Cristobal Island.

Recapture of San Cristóbal Island under Don Fadrique de Toledo by Félix Castelo, 1629. *Courtesy of Wikimedia Commons.*

In 1633, the Tierra Firma fleet, now under the Marquis of Cadereyta, continued pirate hunting. The fleet surprised six corsair vessels at the island of San Bartolome, and they took one. A few days later, they were at their chief target, San Martin Island, which was defended by Dutch soldiers and their black slaves. As the galleons bombarded the fort, troops were landed, and they attacked the fort from the rear, forcing it to surrender. Cadereyta garrisoned the fort and then moved on to New Spain, having continued the use of a galiflota to corner pirates.

By 1685, Spanish naval objectives had recognized the value of the San Sebastian privateers by including Cantabrian ships in the Indies. Guipuzcoan shipowners prepared a fleet of frigates to fight pirates in the Indies, even though they could not directly trade there. The Indies War Council negotiated a contract with San Sebastian shipowners to prepare the fleet specifically against English pirates. Three priests from San Telmo were also given a place in the fleet since many Guipuzcoan sailors could not understand the Spanish language. The construction of this fleet was carried out with great speed in the Anoeta shipyard at San Sebastian. It comprised the flagship *Nuestra Señora del Rosario y Animas*, which weighed 250 tons and had thirty-five cannons; the vice admiral's 140-ton ship, *San Nicolás de Bari*; and the tenders *San Antonio* and *Santiago*. These ships were manned by 437 men. Once they had reached American waters, they fought against English pirates around infamous Tortuga Island. They were not successful, but at least the San Sebastian shipowners and privateers were now involved in the Spanish effort against the Indies pirates.

In sum, to combat pirates and its enemies, sixteenth-century Spanish authorities developed fleets of merchant vessels and galleons to carry goods to the Indies and return with its wealth of bullion and treasure. These fleets, however, were gathered only for the duration of a voyage; in fact, no permanent Spanish navy existed until the early seventeenth century, when Philip III and Philip IV established a permanent Spanish Navy. Laws were passed to protect Spanish shipping by using privateers. The reforms included a tax to support the navy, the establishment of state-of-the-art shipyards, efforts by galleons to take on pirates in their own Caribbean lairs and privateering. Near the end of the century, Cantabrian privateer ports like San Sebastian were allowed to put together fleets to combat pirates in the Indies.

Chapter Three
Menéndez de Aviles and Francis Drake

A CORSAIRING ASTURIAN ADMIRAL

In 1565, Pedro Menéndez de Aviles was given the title of adelantado by Philip II and was sent to the Florida coast to drive out the French Huguenots, who had settled the year before at Fort Caroline, near present-day Jacksonville. In late August, Menéndez established a base to the south at the site of St. Augustine. Meanwhile, Huguenot Jean Ribault had arrived with a superior French fleet to reinforce the French Florida colony, and upon word of Menéndez's presence, Ribault decided to attack him. However, stormy weather intervened, and Ribault's fleet was forced below St. Augustine and wrecked. Under cover of the storm, Menéndez moved north toward Fort Caroline, surprising the garrison and easily taking it. He had the defenders massacred because they were "Lutheran" heretics, and this was the beginning of a week of disaster for the French. South of St. Augustine, 150 people were put to the sword, and the place would come to be named *Matanzas*, Spanish for slaughter. Finally, Ribault and the remains of his force were put to the knife. The enterprise of the French Huguenots had been snuffed out in a bloodbath. Menéndez, however, should not be held entirely responsible for the murders: in all fairness, such a barren and unsettled coast lacked the resources required for Menéndez to feed and care for prisoners.

What background and talents did Menéndez bring to the Florida endeavor? He was an Asturian, brought up along the Cantabrian coast of northern Spain, which was one of the great shipbuilding and seafaring regions of Spain. As a sailor, he had first gained experience in his own patax, warding off French privateers that haunted the Cantabrian coast. By 1550, he had gone to the Indies as master of a commercial vessel with a letter of marque from Charles V. He would become a fleet general with a reputation for making rapid returns to Spain with private and royal treasure. He built ships in Vizcaya, and while the monopoly at Seville shut out Cantabria from direct trade with America, he and his family engaged in smuggling and spent time in the jail of the Casa de la Contratacíon for their illegal activities. Menéndez himself smuggled bullion into Spain.

Still, Philip II regarded Menéndez as the man for the job of settling Florida. He provided him with a three-year contract as adelantado of Florida—"lord of the marches"—and was charged to found, fortify and populate at least two cities, as well as explore and defend his land. Menéndez already saw that control of the shallow coastal waters where fortified ports met inland rivers was the key to Spanish success in the Americas. With these obligations, he would enlist a hundred farmers as settlers, carefully noting the skills of his soldiers, which included twenty-one tailors and sixteen carpenters. He was named an admiral, governor and captain general of Florida. The king would

Pedro Menéndez de Aviles by Francisco de Paula Marti, 1791. *Courtesy Library of Congress.*

back the venture, financially supplementing Menéndez's extended family of seafaring relatives. Separate fleets would be fitted out in Asturias, the Basque Provinces and Cadiz, meeting at the Canary Islands for the voyage to the Caribbean and the onward to Florida.

Privateers were not lacking in sixteenth-century Spain, especially in Cantabria, Menéndez's homeland. Most of the mariners on the galleons, the naval portion of the carreras, came from there. They chiefly raided French and English ships in the Biscay area. In the Basque Provinces, Antón de Garay started privateering at the end of the fifteenth century in the Atlantic and later continued pirating along the coasts of the New World, for which he was executed. Juan Martinez de Elduayen, from the San Sebastian area, did the same in 1480. He captured three pinnaces that were carrying French merchandise, using the letters of marque he was carrying. The Catholic Kings warned him that this affair had been solved a long time ago. He later attacked a vessel from Bilbao in San Sebastian with the help of his relations. He was again reprimanded by the monarchs, who took his prisoners away from him and made him sign an obligation and pay a fine.

In 1553, Philip II recommended that the San Sebastian shipowners set out to catch some French corsair ships, which were bringing stolen goods back to France from the Caribbean. However, using the king's permission, the shipowners continued attacking French ships, and, on seeing this, the ships that were bringing supplies to Guipuzcoa stopped coming. A year later, four corsair captains from San Sebastian sailed up different French canals and rivers, capturing several merchant ships and taking prisoners from enemy corsairs to the provincial prisons. The four corsairs penetrated into the Bordeaux Estuary with six ships, assaulting and stealing from the surrounding villages. They returned to San Sebastian with forty-two French ships full of artillery and merchandise. Domingo de Albistur took over nine large French ships on their way back from Newfoundland, loaded with cod and arms. In addition, he took charge of forty-nine French ships loaded with cod and cannons. Of the four corsairs, it was perhaps Domingo de Iturain who was most famous. He started with a small ship, taking a larger and better armed ship prisoner, with which he specialized in stealing the catches taken by British fishing ships in Newfoundland. The attacks by the San Sebastian corsairs continued until 1559, when peace was signed with France. This was the background for Menéndez's exploits in Florida.

With its French threat gone, Menéndez could now work to establish communities. From the time of the Reconquest of Spanish territory from the Moslems, Spaniards had viewed colonization in terms of the founding

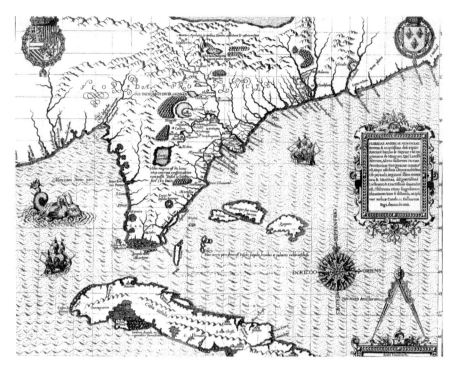

Map of Florida by Jacques Le Moyne and Theodor de Bray, 1591. *Courtesy of Wikimedia Commons.*

of cities rather than land grants. Hence, no matter how small and miserable a settlement was, it was treated formally as a city with a cabildo, or city council, to govern it. St. Augustine was the first place Menéndez landed ammunition, and he took possession of the vast expanse of Florida from there. Actually, following his instructions as adelantado, Menéndez would found three cities—not just St. Augustine but also San Mateo, the former Fort Caroline and Santa Elena, in what became South Carolina. San Mateo burned, and the fort was rebuilt, but the men at both it and St. Augustine would soon be starving, as Menéndez left to return to Spain and bring back settlers in the spring to found Santa Elena.

When he returned the next year, he made St. Elena's most northern post, its fine harbor, the capital of Florida, while St. Augustine and San Mateo were equal satellites. After he started receiving a subsidy from Philip II, he named a deputy governor and garrisons and set up cabildos. At the St. Augustine settlement, several wood forts succeeded each other, and a village was established, following the grid pattern recommended by the 1563

36

Ordinances for Town Planning. But San Mateo was attacked by French privateer Dominique de Gourgues, and it was so devastated that it had to be abandoned. Menéndez continued to bolster Santa Elena with more farmers from Galicia, and he asked that members of his family be given governmental offices so that persons of noble blood would be attracted to Florida. However, Menéndez died in 1574 at the shipyards of Santander before seeing the full fruits of his labor. Two years later, Indians devastated the Santa Elena settlement, and although it was rebuilt, St. Augustine's ability to endure attacks caused it to become the capital of Florida.

A CORSAIRING DEVONSHIRE ADMIRAL

At the beginning of the sixteenth century, England paled as a naval power when compared to Venice, let alone Spain. By the end of the century, however, England had the best fighting fleet in Europe. This fleet grew in concert with privateer enterprise. Queen Elizabeth I pretended to the Spanish that she could do nothing to stop her independent-minded but licensed privateers. She tolerated them because they provided a ready source of revenue for her island state and made up most of her fleets from private sources because she could not afford the expense of the navy. When Francis Drake set sail for the Strait of Magellan in 1577 (eventually raiding Peru and the west Spanish coast before becoming the first English sailor to circumnavigate the world), his return booty was sufficient to enable Elizabeth to pay off the entire national debt. Drake was given £10,000 for himself. His crew

Sir Francis Drake at Buckland Abbey by M. Gheeraerts, 1592. *Courtesy City of Plymouth Museums and Art Gallery.*

got nothing of the prize money, a situation showing he was a privateer, not a pirate.

Drake came from Devonshire, the west coast of England. Devonshire was, as aforementioned, a home of adventurers, sailors and privateers that were regarded by enemy states as pirates. Members of well-established Devon country families, especially younger sons, as well as parish gentry, were attracted to the business of plunder. Sometimes the connection involved no more than raiding ships, but the enterprise was profitable. The coast of Devon was full of harbors, such as the River Dart, which emptied at Dartmouth, or where the rivers Plym and Tamar joined at Plymouth. In the midst of the Bristol Channel, the infamous Lundy Island was at the entrance to one of England's greatest ports. Since the Middle Ages, the island had been occupied by Spanish, French and Barbary, as well as English, pirates.

At age twenty-three, Drake made his first voyage to America, sailing with his second cousin, Sir John Hawkins, in a fleet of ships owned by his relatives, the Hawkins family of Plymouth. In 1568, he was again with a Hawkins fleet when it was trapped by the Spaniards in the Mexican port of San Juan de

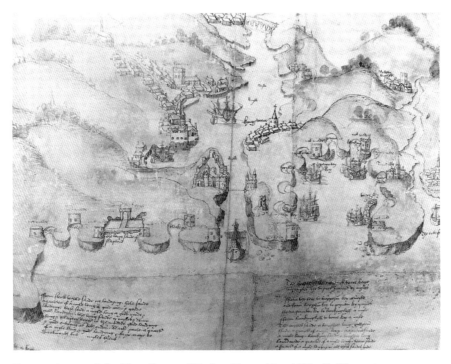

Panoramic map of the River Dart and Torbay, Devonshire, 1539–40. The entire coast was a nursery ground for sailors. *Courtesy the Public Record Office and the British Museum.*

Ulua. He escaped along with Hawkins, but the experience is said to have led him into his lifelong revenge against the Spanish.

Drake would be labeled a pirate by the Spaniards for three reasons: he waged a private war against the king of Spain; Elizabeth I, the astute diplomat, often claimed she knew nothing of what he was doing; and he chose to capture prizes of great profit rather than follow the rules of reason of state. In some ways, Drake was not a pirate, for he was not cooperative with his crew or captains. He worked on his own. He was not loved by his men or his captains. When he landed at Plymouth, they deserted in droves. Drake never lost his confidence as he waged his private war against Philip II. He had some glorious homecomings because of the prizes he took. While Elizabeth lent him ships for his ventures, she denied responsibility for his behavior. The notion that a private person, a simple knight, could be at war with the greatest king in Christendom belonged in a romance of chivalry. His self-confidence transcended ordinary sanity. In the Spanish view, that made Francis Drake a pirate.

Elizabeth also came to treat him as a pirate. After 1589, she put him aside because he was no longer invincible and as she put it, "he went to

Elizabeth I of England in The Pelican Portrait attributed to Nicholas Hillard, circa 1578. That year, Drake circumnavigated the globe aboard a ship named the *Pelican*. *Courtesy of Wikimedia Commons.*

places more for profit than for service." The queen continued to benefit as a partner in many of these voyages, but she represented the state treasury. Moreover, he began to fail in his exploits in the early 1590s.

Drake Sacks St. Augustine

September 14, 1585, Drake began a typical voyage with seven large ships and twenty-two smaller vessels, sailing from Plymouth. The fleet stopped at Bayonne and Vigo on the northwest coast of Spain and reached Santiago in the Cape Verde Islands on November 17. That town was plundered and burned, and on November 29, the fleet set sail across the Atlantic. On New Year's Day, 1586, they reached Santo Domingo, which was captured and plundered, and they issued a 25,000 ducat ransom. By February 9, Cartagena was captured and was occupied until March 26. Here again, the town was plundered, and a ransom of 110,000 ducats was collected.

His fleet then sailed north across the Caribbean to Cuba and then to Florida, where after cruising along the coast for some time, they discovered, on May 28, a beacon-like Spanish watchtower, probably at Matanzas. Unbeknownst to them at the time, they were south of St. Augustine. The city had matured since the time of the adelantado. The Menéndez family continued to hold the position of governor. They had gained the privilege of sending one ship of exports annually to Spain, free from regulations of the Casa de la Contratacíon. The Menéndezes no longer sent Spanish farmers to settle the area, but the community grew as members of the garrison married and remained. A church and fishnets now added to the domestic tranquility of the town. At the time, Pedro Menéndez Márquez, nephew of the adelantado, was governor of Florida.

Drake's men manned their pinnaces, came ashore and began to march along the Matanzas River, still uncertain of who occupied the area. Drake and his second in command, Christopher Carleill, marched with them until they spied the wooden Spanish fort at St. Augustine, and about a mile above it, "a little town or village without walls, built of wooden houses." Drake's men had artillery, and they prepared themselves to bombard the fort. A scout of perhaps a dozen men under Carleill was sent out at night to reconnoiter the fort. When the garrison discovered them, they assumed it was the entire army, and unknown to the English, most abandoned the fort. A French prisoner in the fort came to them in a boat, playing on this fife, "the tune of the Prince of Orange," and told them that the garrison had left. The English then came in force and met with little opposition, taking over the fort.

Within the walls, what most concerned Drake's raiders was the "thirteen or fourteen great pieces of brass ordnance, and a chest...having in it the value of some two thousand pounds sterling"—most likely the king's coffer. The fort was burned. The town was next, and after little resistance, was in their hands, although at the loss of one of Drake's best officers, Captain Anthony Powell. The impoverished settlement was then sacked, adding little to what was taken at the fort. The governor, Menéndez Márquez, was not found. Indians and blacks did create a brief diversion in front of Drake's camp.

By May 31, Drake had left, moving north toward Roanoke Island, Virginia, a settlement established by Sir Walter Raleigh that was floundering from

Coffer with three locks, 1537. This coffer belonged to the Casa de la Contratacíon in Seville and contained money and goods. *Courtesy Archivo General de Indias, Seville.*

starvation. It was the only colonial toehold the English could afford in America. England lacked the resources for colonization and Drake took the handful of settlers back with him. Drake reached Portsmouth Harbor on July 22.

Drake's raid on St. Augustine was unique. It was by far the largest fleet that St. Augustine would experience, at a time when the town was still struggling to exist. Drake apparently did not know of its existence and more or less stumbled upon it. Almost a century would pass before another such attack was made on St. Augustine. Drake did establish the precedent of attacking the presidio from the south, up the Matanzas River, largely by marching, supplemented by small craft. This allowed them to avoid the treacherous sand bar at the entrance to St. Augustine's harbor, which could only be navigated at high tide with a pilot. Without such aid, Drake's large ships would never have been able to enter the harbor. Finally, as a result of Drake's sacking the city, it was decided that Santa Elena, once the capital of the adelantado's vast domain, be abandoned because it could not be defended against pirates like Drake.

Expeditions like Drake's would become obsolete due to the rise of the Royal Navy by the mid-seventeenth century, which reduced the role privateers had played in the Elizabethan navy. The private adventurer was an annoyance to the new navy, competing as it did for the same manpower. Targets for Devon adventurers moved closer to home as they drifted away from the Iberian coast and focused mainly on the English Channel and the North Sea. The days of Drake, the Elizabethan navy and the Lundy pirates were soon over.

Of the two great sailors, Menéndez and Drake, the latter had a much narrower purpose in his course of action. His single objective was to gain booty for his investors, of which the capture of St. Augustine's coffer and cannon were his only justification for deviating off course. Drake had to show a profit for his private investors; hence, Spaniards found him to be a pirate. Menéndez was as bloodthirsty as Drake in exterminating the French Huguenots, and his family also engaged in smuggling (a necessity because of Seville's monopoly over Indies trade). However, he gave far more financially than he made. He was genuinely concerned to settle Florida and Christianize its Indians.

Drake was the first so-called pirate to attack St. Augustine, leaving the lingering impression that most pirates were Englishmen. In fact, pirate crews were usually of mixed origin, and a century later, French-led pirate raids against St. Augustine would be more prominent than English. In the second half of the seventeenth century, it would be the resourceful expanding monarchy of Louis XIV of France that would be a common threat to Spain and England, forcing them to be allies.

Chapter Four
Pirate Attacks

From the 1660s to the 1680s, the West Indies was in turmoil as privateers became pirates and disregarded the alliances created in Europe. The Spanish empire remained a target of French, English and Dutch traders and raiders, occasionally supported by a formal fleet from their homeland. It was not a good time for Spain, as it was at an end of a long decline that had begun in the mid-seventeenth century. During these years, the nation was on the defensive, depending on the erection of masonry fortifications rather than naval power to sustain its colonies. The policy would not even reach St. Augustine until the 1670s, when the building of Castillo San Marcos was finally begun and continued over several decades. Until then, makeshift and dilapidated wooden fortifications made do. The forts had uses beyond defense. A drawing of the fort in 1593 shows it also to be a warehouse and administrative center. Even when the Castillo was finally completed in the 1694, the village below it remained easily occupied and sacked by an enemy, so that it had to develop its own protective earthen walls.

The years 1660 to 1690 marked the beginning of a golden age of piracy. War in America was unbroken and largely economic. The Spanish flotas were rarely targeted by the English, French and Dutch pirates, because the odds were too great. Instead, raids on colonial outposts like St. Augustine were executed by either privateers outfitted for profit by merchants and nobles or a combination of state and private financing. These fleets targeted Spain's poorly defended settlements like St. Augustine and either pillaged them or demanded ransom, which was often paid in goods and slaves.

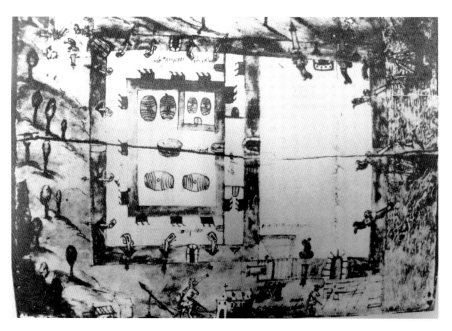

Detail of 1593 plan of St. Augustine's fort and warehouse. *Courtesy Archivo General de Indias, Seville.*

The only time that St. Augustine held coinage was when the annual situado subsidy, collected in Mexico, arrived there from Vera Cruz via Havana. It provided support for St. Augustine's Franciscans, presents for Indian chiefs and supplies such as flour, salt, wax, wine, medicine and cloth purchased in Mexico or Havana—but the lion's share went to pay the garrison and its dependents.

The golden age of piracy appeared in St. Augustine when Englishmen Robert Searles led a raid on the city in 1668. Little is known of Robert Searles's (alias John Davis) early life. His career was constantly interrupted by quarrels with Sir Thomas Modyford, the English governor of Jamaica. Searles's first known ship was the eight-gun *Cagway*, which he captained as a privateer in 1663 from Jamaica to the south coast of Cuba, along with a force of 1,300 men and under the direction of the Royal Navy's Sir Christopher Myngs. The fleet aimed to take the privateer port of Santiago de Cuba. It was sacked, and Searles returned to Jamaica with his booty. The south coast of Cuba remained open to attacks by English raiders because of its proximity to Jamaica.

Other raids led Spanish authorities to protest that Jamaica was a center of English piracy. Charles II ordered Modyford to forbid piracy by punishing the culprits and restoring the property taken. In reaction, Searles had taken two rich Cuban ships, and they were sitting in Port Royal Harbor when news of the new policy arrived. The governor's council decided to return the prizes and to take Searles's commission, rudder and sails, which essentially put him out of business. Searles, however, escaped. He would serve with Colonel Edward Morgan, brother of the notorious privateer turned pirate Henry Morgan, in a force of reformed privateers, giving up their piracy. To the governor, the force was a bargain because it only cost the king powder and mortars when it took St. Eustatius in 1666. Searles then decided to cruise to the Cuban coast and base himself among the Bahamas's pirates. He witnessed the Spanish raid of the pirate base at New Providence a year later. Like most of his compatriots, he hoped to catch a straggler from the New Spain flota out of Havana. But this did not materialize and, rather than return to Jamaica empty-handed, the pirates resolved to retaliate against the weak Spanish presidio at St. Augustine. Searles led the enterprise without a commission from anyone and Modyford considered it an act that violated Charles II's orders. While Searles had previously participated as privateer in official English expeditions against Spanish targets, the attack on St. Augustine established him as a pirate.

SEARLES SACKS ST. AUGUSTINE

Searles led a fleet from the Bahamas to sack St. Augustine. He had captured a French surgeon, Pierre Piguet, who turned out to have been St. Augustine's surgeon until 1667, when the governor, Francisco de la Guerra, had expelled him. Piquet told Searles that silver bars had been recovered from the wreck of a ship, a rare event in normally impoverished St. Augustine. Off the coast of Havana, Searles's fleet captured the Vera Cruz situado ship carrying Mexican flour and bound for St. Augustine. He also took St. Augustine's own frigate. Since both captured ships were expected, the town assumed that they were on a routine return. Governor Guerra ordered his 120 men to rack their matchlocks at the guardhouse and go home to sleep. In fact, the pilot who was sent out to conduct the ships into the bay was taken prisoner when he stepped aboard the supply ship. The inhabitants would have little warning and were not able to flee as they had when Drake appeared almost a century before.

At 1:00 a.m., on May 29, over a hundred of Searles's men began rowing in launches and piraguas across Matanzas Bay. Corporal Miguel de Monzon was fishing in the bay and discovered them, and they wounded him as he rowed toward the town dock to sound the alarm. He shouted warnings in the town as he reached the city's wooden fort. The guardhouse was overrun by the pirates as the outnumbered guards fled to the fort. Many of the citizens were killed as their homes were looted. Sergeant Major Nicolás Ponce de León, senior officer of the garrison, rose from his sickbed to shepherd 130 bewildered men, women and children—including 70 unarmed soldiers—to the safety of the surrounding woods. Governor Guerra escaped from the government house and safely reached the wooden fort. The fort was not yet the impressive Castillo it is today but rather a rotting wooden structure just to the south. Adjutant Isidro de Reinoso notified Captain Mateo Pacheco Salgado of Searles's approach. The gate was opened to let in the town guard, the governor and other royal officials and a few citizens. The governor took command of 33 men and distributed ammunition from the powder magazine.

Before the fort's cannons were loaded, Searles attacked. The fighting continued for an hour and a half with Searles's men aiming at the glowing match cords of the Spanish musketeers. Five defenders were killed and five more wounded. But Searles's losses were considerable at eleven dead and nineteen wounded. During the respite, the governor was able to strengthen his position as messengers were sent urging everyone to come to the fort. By the morning of May 29, Ponce led seventy weaponless men into the fort.

Searles now brought his own ship, the *Cagway*, and the two captured Spanish ships into Matanzas Bay, despite the fire from the fort. The privateers had stripped the king's coffer, the royal warehouses, the hospital, the parish church and the Franciscan convent chapel. They also took the royal treasurer, José de Prado, hostage. The booty was systematically gathered in the town and would be placed on the *Cagway* and the Vera Cruz ship.

In the afternoon, the governor charged out of the fort and tried to drive the marauders out. But when his troops began to suffer casualties, the governor brought them back to the fort. Still, the privateers had had enough and left the next morning, having spent twenty hours in the presidio. In all, sixty citizens and soldiers were dead. Searles held about seventy prisoners of both sexes and offered to ransom them for water, meat and wood for his return voyage. Governor Guerra accepted, but he wanted the flour from the Vera Cruz ship to remain.

The women and other captives were released. Over six days, the ransom was paid and the prisoners were returned, although the pirates wanted to keep the Indians, blacks and even mestizos for sale as slaves in Jamaica.

They claimed they were authorized to do this by Modyford, an obvious falsehood. Most of these people were free in St. Augustine, and Searles's claim that they were slaves was a terrible violation of Hispanic society. This would not be the last time that pirates claimed the right to sell citizens of St. Augustine as slaves.

The fort had not been conquered, and Spanish resistance had been fierce, although the town was sacked. The pirates did not actually burn the fort, a sign that they had enough information about the place to return and establish a base to capture more vessels trading in the Indies.

In the aftermath, the parish priest, Francisco de Sotolongo, laid the blame for the disaster on Governor Guerra. The charge had nothing to do with his conduct against the pirates. The bachelor governor had kept a mistress in his house for three years. It made no difference that, as a royal appointee, he was forbidden to marry into a local family during his term. He had fallen in love with Lorenza de Soto y Aspiolea, who bore him three illegitimate children. The priest saw this sin as having incurred God's wrath, so that the privateers were sent to punish his city.

Searles was able to release the English doctor, Henry Woodward, from the Spanish, and he became the surgeon of the privateers. After his St. Augustine expedition, Searles returned to Jamaica, but he had to avoid Port Royal for a while. He was finally apprehended by Modyford and placed in jail. He was released to serve with Henry Morgan's 1671 expedition that ended in the vicious sacking of Panama. There, Morgan would reproach Searles for failing to capture a plate galleon, which was a sitting duck, because his men were too drunk to take it. He died obscurely on an expedition to the Gulf of Campeche, supposedly to cut logwood. His career shows how easily a privateer captain could become a pirate, as he violated the rules of war and became an outlaw in Jamaica.

The Castillo and Pirates of 1683–84

To prevent further pirate depredations and to offset the founding of Charles Town, South Carolina, Spanish authorities decided to provide the town with a masonry fortress. In Spain, Queen Maria, the regent for Charles II, and her councilors aided St. Augustine by ordering New Spain's viceroy to add fifty soldiers to the garrison, increasing the situado accordingly and constructing a new fort. Governor Guerra had also written a letter to the viceroy asking for fifty of the latest flintlock muskets so that he could better defend the presidio.

Drawing of work on the east wall of Castillo San Marcos, 1675. *Courtesy of Eastern National Parks & Monument Association.*

On July 6, 1671, Sergeant Major Manuel de Cendoya arrived in St. Augustine to be governor and captain general of Florida. His principal duty was to begin the construction of Castillo San Marcos. On August 8, he opened quarries on Anastasia Island, from which coquina stone was extracted. More than a year later, the first shovelful of dirt on foundation trenches was dug, followed by the first stone laid at the site. Indian peons from Florida and black slaves from Cuba would be imported to provide most of the labor for the fortification. It would take twenty-three years to complete the project.

Even after the Castillo construction was underway, St. Augustine would be the target of pirate attacks. The appearance of French captains in these pirate attacks was a sign that Spain's chief enemy was now Louis XIV's France, and such initiatives would lead Sebastian Vauban to affirm the value of French privateers.

Realizing the strength of the new fortress, these pirates sought another way of entering Matanzas Bay rather than over the sand bar, probing the Matanzas Inlet and River south of St. Augustine as Drake had done. The next pirate expedition was formed without the knowledge of the Bahamas's governor Roger Clarke. The pirates gained provisions in Charles Town, South Carolina, by sending a silver bar to the city worth 1,000 pesos. Initially, the pirates had been interested in salvaging a sunken Spanish treasure ship using Florida Indian divers. They sent canoes to find natives who knew the location of the sunken ship, but they ran into a Spanish privateer out of Havana, captained by Juan de Iriarte. Captain Iriarte was able to sink one of their canoes and take one French and several English pirates prisoner, returning with them to Havana.

In late February 1683, Florida's governor, Juan Márquez Cabrera, had received warning from Havana by way of San Marcos de Apalache and from Indians to the south of St. Augustine that French and English pirates from the Bahamas intended to attack the presidio. Governor Cabrera took defensive measures, erecting two new, coastal watchtowers, one at Ayamón, about twenty-seven miles south of the presidio, and another on the beach north of the town. Summoning the citizenry into the safety of the partially completed Castillo, he stationed his garrison and militia troops at likely landing places.

The Florida coast was approached in March 1683 by the mixed fleet of French and English ships, which landed nearly three hundred pirates seventy miles south of St. Augustine. They were flying the French colors on *La Fortune* and were led by French captain Abraham Bréhal. Other pirate vessels were English ships, a six-gun frigate under Captain Jeremiah Canoe, a sloop under Captain George Younge and the ships of Captains Jan Corneliszoon, John Markham, Thomas Paine and Conway Woolley.

Captain Thomas Paine was a resident of Rhode Island, who had been separately commissioned by Jamaica's governor, Sir Thomas Lynch, to seek and destroy pirates. He instead joined other privateers under Bréhal in 1683; Bréhal held a French privateer's commission from the governor of Saint Domique. Paine's eight-gun bark, the *Pearl*, sailed under the French flag in this Florida raid. After the raid on St. Augustine, he returned to Jamaica, where he was detained by the governor for violating England's peace treaty with Spain, but his and Bréhal's ships were able to get away to the Bahamas.

There, the hapless governor, Robert Lilburne, tried to detain the privateers but had no force to do this. They then returned to Paine's Rhode Island home, where the governor accused them of having counterfeit papers, but he and Bréhal were released and Paine remained at home. Clearly, raiders like Paine and Bréhal were pirates in the eyes of English governors, but they lacked the ability or will to prosecute them.

On March 30, 1683, the pirates marched north along the beach with two pirogues for use in the water until they spied the watchtower at Matanzas Inlet. They had with them St. Augustine renegade Alonso de Avecilla as their forced guide. Avecilla had been living in the Bahamas, where they had forced him to accompany the expedition. Under the cover of darkness, some of the invaders crept up behind the tower and surprised the five sentries, who were asleep. They tortured the soldiers for information on the town's defenses. But the pirates had been seen by a corporal before they reached the tower, and a warning message was sent to the presidio. The next day, the pirates continued their march on St. Augustine. Aware of their presence, Governor Cabrera dispatched Captain Antonio de Argüelles with

Matanzas watchtower, as described by Governor Manuel de Cendoya, 1671. *Drawing by Albert Manucy. Courtesy of St. Augustine Historical Society.*

forty musketeers to ambush them. Eight miles from the town, the pirates walked into a withering fire and, after a few exchange shots (one of which lodged in Argüelles' leg), they beat a hasty retreat back to their boats and then to their ships.

A militia company of forty-eight free pardos (mulattos) and morenos (blacks), under command of African blacksmith Lieutenant Juan Merino, were able to stop the pirates. The company's establishment had been a result of not only Cabrera's shortage of manpower but also of the insult that Searles had perpetrated by treating the black freedmen as slaves. Merino was from Havana and was exiled for a crime to St. Augustine in 1675. In St. Augustine, he was a charcoal burner in the royal forge, repairing weapons for the military. When the freedmen company was formed, he already owned his own forge, so that was a position to arm the new company.

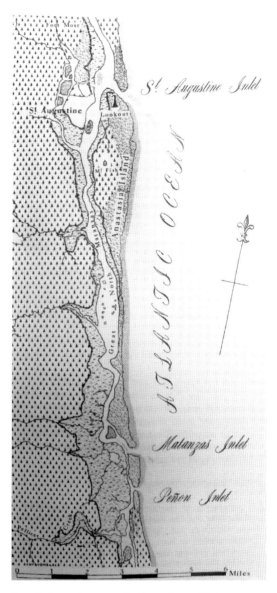

Detail of map between St. Augustine and Matanzas Inlets, adapted from William Gerard de Brahm's map. *Map by Charles S. Coomes, 1769. Courtesy of St. Augustine Historical Society.*

His corporal was Crispin de Tapia, who was a free mulatto who managed a store. Such black militia also had the possibility of becoming garrison seamen or soldiers.

Expecting the worst from the pirates, the residents of the presidio crowded into the Castillo. Cabrera, his soldiers, the men and even the women of the town worked day and night to strengthen the unfinished Castillo, which still did not have quarters or ovens within the walls. Missing parapets and firing steps were improvised from dry stone. Except for a few sentries, the town was abandoned.

By April 5, the pirates had brought their ships from Matanzas to the sand bar at the entrance to St. Augustine's harbor, where they threatened the Castillo. Seeing the town alerted and the Castillo at arms, however, the pirates were not willing to risk the bar and decided to abandon their St. Augustine enterprise. The town was not sacked, and the unfinished Castillo had discouraged the pirates from further assault. Instead, they raided the easier prey to the north at Spanish Guale on the Florida-Georgia coast. They sacked the coastal mission villages of San Juan del Puerto and Santa María. At San Simons Island, they carried off provisions, church bells and ornaments and killed the Indians. After careening their vessels on the Isla de San Pedro, the pirates buried their dead. They continued to devastate the exposed Spanish missions north of St. Augustine.

St. Augustine's Franciscan friars and Pablo de Hita Salazar, veteran soldier and the previous governor, criticized Governor Cabrera's handling of the defense. He was accused of not following up on the skirmishes his troops won on Anastasia Island and of hiding in the fort when he should have attempted to defend the town. It was claimed the citizens had been allowed to stay in the Castillo for too long after the pirates had left, preventing the garrison from carrying out its duties. Even the formation of the company of pardos and morenos was frowned upon by Salazar, because he had experienced them as recruits for the regular army and thought them too enterprising to make decent soldiers. Second-guessing like this was something that all of St. Augustine's governors had to endure.

Having found St. Augustine a tough nut to crack, pirate raids, in 1684, continued to focus on the missions to the north. On September 30, six Anglo-French pirate vessels landed near the St. Johns River led by Englishman Andrew Ransom. They were defeated by Spanish troops, and Governor Cabrera condemned them to labor on the Castillo with the exception of Ransom, who was sentenced to be garroted. However, Ransom was a Catholic and, when the silk cord around his neck broke, the Franciscans claimed it was "an act of God," and he fled to the priory where the friars refused to give him up. The governor continued his feud with the Franciscans, and he commuted Ransom's sentence to the same labor as his crew. Ransom thus managed to avoid the garroting feared by all pirates.

Nicholas Grammont (Agramónt)

This respite from pirates did not last. On May 1, 1686, a famous pirate, Frenchman Nicholas Grammont, appeared at St. Augustine, a place that he assumed would be an easy target. Known for his gambling and haughty manner, Grammont was a notoriously successful pirate, having seized major treasures and captured several Caribbean forts and ports.

Le Chevalier Nicholas Grammont was born in 1643 in Paris, the son of a king's guard, and began his career at sea with the French Royal Marines. He was actually forced to go to sea because of a tragic duel with his sister's suitor. The suitor died from wounds sustained in the duel, ruining Grammont's reputation, so that he had to leave France. He eventually gained command of a frigate and acted as a privateer. His new status as a captain paid off in the capture of a rich Dutch convoy. After his ship was wrecked by a storm, he decided to put aside privateering and turn to piracy, moving his base of operations to the notorious pirate base, Tortuga Island.

On Tortuga, he used the convoy's riches to outfit a new ship with fifty guns. With his reputation as a successful captain, he had no trouble recruiting a crew. In 1678, although a pirate, he joined the ill-fated French expedition under the Comte d'Estrïes on the fleet's voyage to Curacao, where it was wrecked on the reef. The misfortune created a vacuum in French naval power that allowed pirates like Grammont to thrive. Without the might of a French fleet to aid them, the pirates still had nineteen remaining ships and chose Maracaibo, Venezuela, as a likely target. Grammont landed his force there in June and was able to capture it. The pirates plundered the whole region and did not depart until the end of the year, when they returned to Tortuga as heroes.

Grammont joined forces with Laurens de Graff, a cultured French pirate, who was known in St. Augustine because he had been married in the Canary Islands. They attacked Vera Cruz brutally in May 1683, herding the city's populace into its cathedral while they plundered and left the citizens to perish without food or water. After days of looting, the pirates fled the area to avoid the twelve men-of-war of the Spanish plate fleet. Later, the pirates reunited and determined to raid Campeche on the Yucatan Peninsula, a city that had trade connections with St. Augustine. The pirates attacked in July 1685, and after several days of fighting, they finally succeeded in snuffing out resistance. The citizens, however, had hidden their treasure elsewhere and after two months of sacking with few results, Grammont sent a demand for ransom to the governor, who ignored it. Grammont then commenced to execute prisoners in retaliation for the affront. De Graff did stop the executions, and the pirates finally departed Campeche. Certainly Grammont had gained the reputation in Vera Cruz and Campeche of being a butcher.

Considering Grammont's record, taking St. Augustine seemed to be no challenge. After waiting for English pirates who did not appear, he joined another Frenchman, Captain Nicholas Brigaut, and they formed their own expedition. Brigaut would command the pirates on land, with Grammont dominating the fleet. While Grammont's ships remained to the south of St. Augustine, Brigaut landed eighty men at the south end of Anastasia Island on April 30, 1686, seizing the first watchtower at Ayamót and moving north toward Matanzas Inlet. But Brigaut was observed by the other watchtower, and the city was warned. St. Augustine governor Juan Márquez Cabrera appointed José Begambre to head twenty-five infantry to foil Brigaut's advance, but they failed. Another force of fifty men under Captain Antonio de Arguelles attacked the pirates in hand-to-hand fighting just south of Matanzas Inlet. They succeeded with the support of black militia and local Indians, forcing Brigaut to retreat southward, and he sent a message to Grammont that he needed help. Brigaut had left his galliot aground and attempted a rendezvous with Grammont to the south at Mosquito Inlet. On the way, however, his force was intercepted by the garrison and massacred, the only survivors being Brigaut, a black freebooter named Diego, and a nine-year-old boy. On May 31, Brigaut and Diego were executed by garroting in St. Augustine's plaza. Thus, Grammont was left without an army.

Grammont knew nothing of Brigaut's demise, and he headed up the coast in his ships to the inlet at St. Augustine's harbor. From there, he hoped to blockade and starve St. Augustine into surrender. When the townspeople heard of his presence, they barricaded themselves inside the Castillo. The citizens believed the pirates were waiting to seize ships carrying the situado from Havana. Grammont's ships stayed in the area searching for Brigaut's men. The blockade was maintained for sixteen days but finally abandoned as Grammont gave up hope of finding Brigaut's men and sailed north to take on provisions. Somewhere off the coast of Guale, Grammont and his hands were reportedly lost in a storm. Thus, after his brilliant career as a pirate, he not only failed to capture St. Augustine, but as fate would have it, went down with his ship.

While Grammont's attack was quashed, the fear he inspired drove the governor to finish the Castillo de San Marco without interruption. The aggression by the chiefly French pirates was far from being spontaneous. French authorities encouraged them, and a war between France and Spain was formally declared in 1689. After initial success, French pirates skipped St. Augustine, as they decided the Castillo was too strong. Instead they concentrated on the Florida Keys, which were a stopping place for ships between Havana and Florida. Provision ships were taken at the Keys, causing St. Augustine to face a greater threat than the pirates: starvation. In the years to come, the provisioning of St. Augustine's growing population would force the city's governors to seek every source of food, even supplies from the enemy.

Grammont's and Brigaut's attack was the last pirate expedition against St. Augustine. Some pirates had implied that St. Augustine might be a good base, similar to the isolated but strategically located Bahama Islands. As seen, however, the success rate of the pirates was less than spectacular. Both the protection of the Castillo and the tenacity of the garrison made the place difficult to take. The sand bar at the entrance to the city harbor, as well as the one at Matanzas Inlet, could disrupt land–sea operations. While the possibility of seizing the king's coffer was alluring, the citizens were modest in their fortunes, making the cost of capturing or ransoming the presidio too high. This happened against a background of military conflict, in which English and French authorities saw the raids as means of carrying out war against Spain.

Chapter Five
The Bahamas Pirate "Republic"

The raid of 1683 against St. Augustine had been conducted by pirates using the Bahamas as their base. This chain of islands east of the Florida Channel would be a constant source of concern in St. Augustine. The chief port was Nassau on the island of New Providence. The islands were nominally under English control, but their presence was so weak that pirates often ruled the islands in practice. The proprietors of Carolina, who founded Charles Town, were technically granted responsibility for the Bahamas, but the best they could do for the islands was to appoint an occasional governor. While the names of English pirates ring loudly in accounts of Bahamian piracy, 16 percent of the islands' extensive black male population were mariners and slaves with African backgrounds.

KEEPING THE BAHAMAS IN CHECK

The Bahamas developed by harboring pirates and privateers who preyed on Spanish and French ships. In 1677, the islands' English governor, Roger Clarke, justified privateering as necessary for the colony's defense, but in a letter of marque, he also authorized offensive attacks on Spanish territory far from the Bahamas. Clarke's encouragement of aggressive privateering disregarded the 1667 and 1670 treaties of Madrid, which established peace between England and Spain.

In protecting Florida's and Cuba's coasts, Spaniards had not been passive and attacked the Bahamas in 1667, when Searles was there, and again in

1684. During the War of the Spanish Succession, Cuban-based expeditions in 1703 and 1706, in alliance with the French, would occupy the Bahamas. British governors and most of the island's African slaves were carried off in these raids, and survivors were forced to live in the woods. When new governors arrived, they found the colony deserted. The effect of these attacks was to destroy British control over the Bahamas, but the Spanish and French occupied them only occasionally, so that no state actually controlled them. Here was an opportunity for pirates to fill the vacuum in the Bahamas and remain in proximity to St. Augustine.

Spanish expeditions were sent against the Bahamas at the time pirates were raiding St. Augustine. On January 19, 1684, a Havana-based naval expedition led by corsair Juan de Alarcón sailed against the privateering stronghold of Nassau. With a commission issued by Cuban governor José Fernández de Córdoba, he approached the island of New Providence with a pair of barcos luengos carrying 200 men. Having seized a woodcutting sloop off the island of Andros, he compelled its master, William Bell, to pilot them into the eastern channel, and at daybreak, he disembarked 150 men within a half-mile of Nassau, while his ships bore down upon the six vessels anchored in its harbor.

Nassau's population consisted of approximately four hundred men capable of bearing arms plus perhaps four hundred women and children and two hundred slaves. Surprised, they were incapable of mounting an effective defense. Former governor Robert Clarke was wounded and captured as he attempted to mount a feeble opposition. John Oldmixon, the poet-historian, claimed that Clarke died from being roasted on a spit by the Spanish Inquisition. Others simply say he was made a prisoner.

Clarke's recently arrived successor, Robert Lilburne, fled from his cabin in the *Wheel of Fortune*, along with most other residents. The ten-gun New England frigate *Good Intent*, under Captain William Warren, managed to escape across the bar, leaving the Spaniards to pillage the remaining four ships and quickly ransack the town, loading their plunder aboard their largest prize before torching the rest and sailing away that same evening. Alarcón then went across to Eleuthera Island and destroyed its English settlement before returning to Nassau on November 15, to set fire to its buildings and carry off numerous residents to Havana.

The Spanish expedition reduced the Bahamian settlements and defenses to ruins, and Spaniards carried off many of the inhabitants, depopulating the islands. Some two hundred colonists would seek refuge on Jamaica while another fifty from Eleuthera temporarily resettled in

Maine. The Bahamas subsequently remained devoid of English presence until December 1686, when a small contingent from Jamaica under the preacher Thomas Bridges reoccupied New Providence Island, and more colonists gradually joined them.

1703 and 1706 Destruction

In 1703, a privately raised Franco-Spanish expedition was formed at Santiago de Cuba, inspired by officers who viewed Nassau as a menace. This expedition was led by Blas Moreno Mondragón and Clause Le Chesnaye. Santiago more than matched Havana as a base for privateers because of its location on the south side of Cuba (in the direction of Jamaica) and on the trade winds route to the Gulf Stream. In 1662, Santiago had suffered at the hands of Royal Navy commander Christopher Myngs and pirate Henry Morgan, who had been able to sack it because its Castillo San Pedro de la Roca was not defended. This new joint expedition consisted of French and Spanish soldiers aboard two frigates that attacked Nassau. They surprised the 250 English inhabitants, slaughtered more than 100, seized twenty-two guns, destroyed the fortifications and returned to Santiago a few days later with thirteen prizes and 80 to 100 prisoners. Among them was the governor, Ellis Lightwood.

The English inhabitants retired to the woods until the danger was over. When they returned, they found New Providence completely ruined and decided to go to other settlements. English authorities had neglected the affairs of New Providence and were not aware of the catastrophe. Edward Birch was appointed as the new governor and sent to Nassau, which he found entirely abandoned. He returned home.

Another Franco-Spanish raid in 1706 left only twenty-seven families to survive in makeshift huts on New Providence Island. No more than four hundred to five hundred English residents were scattered in distress, while their overseas trade was at a standstill and no new governors or assistance came from England. Conditions were not much improved twelve years later, when a majority of the population were said to be Spanish refugees. While the Spanish raids had weakened English control over the Bahamas, the adversity of the English population would allow pirates to dominate the Bahamas.

THE PEAK OF THE BAHAMAS PIRACY

Even with British governors in place, the Bahamas became a notorious pirate den. By 1696, the pirate Henry Avery had no trouble in bribing Bahamian governor Nicholas Trott to give his crew refuge. Against a background of imperial rivalry and a lack of commitment from Britain, a "Pirate Republic" would develop in the Bahamas. The peak of pirate activity occurred between 1706 and 1718, when Benjamin Hornigold became "governor" of a pirate republic at Nassau. The fearsome Edward Teach, better known as Blackbeard, was the most famous member of the republic. Henry Jennings, supposedly a privateer operating from Jamaica, was also a leader.

Benjamin Hornigold's early life is unrecorded, but his first acts of piracy were during the winter of 1713–14, when he employed piraguas and a sloop to menace merchant vessels off the coast of New Providence. By 1717, Hornigold had a thirty-gun sloop he named the *Ranger*, which was the most

Drawing of Blackbeard the Pirate. A Bahamian pirate, Blackbeard raided the North Carolina coast until he was killed in 1718 by Joseph Nicholls. *From* A General History of Pirates *by Charles Johnson, circa 1725.*

59

heavily armed ship in the Bahamas, allowing him to seize other vessels. In the spring of that year, he and his lieutenant, Edward Teach, seized three merchant ships in quick succession, one carrying flour bound for Havana, one a Bermudan sloop with a cargo of spirits and one a Portuguese ship with white wine from Madeira. Later, Hornigold attacked an armed merchant vessel sent to the Bahamas by the governor of South Carolina to hunt for pirates. The merchantman escaped by running itself aground, and its captain later reported that Hornigold's fleet had increased to five vessels with a combined crew of around 350.

Hornigold did allow his crew certain "diversions." The passengers of a sloop he captured off the coast of Honduras recounted his men "did us no further injury than the taking most of our hats from us, having got drunk the night before, as they told us, and toss'd theirs overboard."

HORNIGOLD TAKES A PARDON

Despite his supremacy, Hornigold remained careful not to attack British-flagged ships, apparently to maintain a legal fiction that he was a privateer operating against Britain's enemies, even though the War of the Spanish Succession was over. However, his lieutenants disliked this and in November 1717 a vote was taken among the combined crews asserting their right to attack any vessel they chose. Hornigold opposed the decision and was replaced as captain by Edward Teach. Ruthlessly, Teach immediately set sail for the Caribbean, leaving Hornigold to limp back to New Providence in a single sloop with a token crew. He continued piracy from Nassau until December, when word arrived of a general pardon for pirates offered by the king. Hornigold sailed to Jamaica in January 1718 and took the pardon from the governor.

Back in the Bahamas, governor Woodes Rogers granted Hornigold's request for a pardon, but commissioned him to hunt pirates, including his former lieutenant, Edward Teach. For the next eighteen months, Hornigold cruised the Bahamas in pursuit of easier prey like Stede Bonnet, the gentleman pirate, and Jack Rackham. By December 1718, Rogers had written to the Board of Trade in London commending Hornigold's efforts in hunting his former allies. A year later, Hornigold's ship was caught in a hurricane somewhere between New Providence and Mexico and he perished in the wreck. While a pirate he had been, under the Rogers regime, he became a pirate hunter.

CHARLES VANE, JACK RACKHAM AND THE LADIES

Charles Vane was also part of the Pirate "Republic," although he left New Providence in 1718 just as the new governor, Woodes Rogers, arrived. Fearing entrapment by Rogers's fleet, he tried to burn his way out of the harbor behind a fire ship, which forced Rogers's fleet to open a space at Nassau and provide Vane an opportunity to raid the harbor and secure the best pilot. Vane and his crew then escaped in a small sloop at the harbor's narrow entrance. He thus became the only pirate that Rogers did not pardon. He went on to seize prizes in South Carolina. By September, Vane was over one hundred miles north of Nassau, where he was joined by pardoned pirates from New Providence. The next month, Vane met Teach in North Carolina, just before Teach's encounter with the Royal Navy. While at large, Vane was

Engraving of Charles Vane, circa 1720. *Courtesy of Wikimedia Commons.*

a threat to the stability of New Providence and the Carolinas, but eventually he was caught in Jamaica and hanged.

John Rackham was also of the republic and sailed with Vane as quartermaster when they left New Providence. After Vane failed to attack a French man-of-war, however, his crew mutinied, putting Vane in a sloop with a few sailors and naming Rackham commander of Vane's fleet. Like Vane, Rackham was captured in Jamaica by British authorities and executed.

The Bahamian republic also produced rare lady pirates. Anne Bonny, a native of Ireland, came to the Carolinas, where she had an illegitimate daughter with a planter. She then eloped with a sailor and went to New Providence with the daughter she had by him. There, she met John Rackham and became his mistress, going to sea with him in men's clothes. When another child was born, Rackham secretly kept her in Cuba. Her path crossed with another female pirate, Mary Read, and they were friends, causing havoc with Rackham, who thought Read a rival male until he found out their secret. Both women might have been executed as pirates with Rackham but got off because they were pregnant.

Engraving of Anne Bonny (1697–1720), one-time consort of John Rackham. *From Charles Johnson's* A General History of Pirates, *circa 1725.*

THE 1715 WRECK OF THE SPANISH FLOTA

A key event in the rise of piracy in the Bahamas was the wreck of the Carrera de Indies on its way back to Cadiz. In July 1715, the Spanish flota of ten ships left Havana under Captain General Don Juan Esteban, having been much delayed waiting for the Tierra Firma fleet. They needed to be hasty as hurricane season was approaching. They moved north into the Florida Channel between the Bahamas and the mainland. At midnight, a full-fledged hurricane struck, ultimately forcing the ships to the Florida shore where they were broken up and perhaps one thousand seamen drowned, including the captain general. The survivors made camp on the shore, and a ship's boat was sent northward to St. Augustine and arrived in about a week.

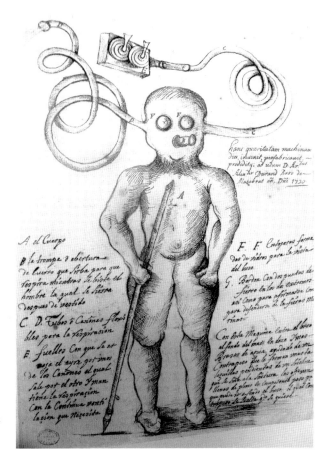

Ideal for salvaging, this primitive diving suit was worn by a man underwater. It is fitted over an iron hood, jerkin and trousers. *Courtesy Archivo General de Indias.*

A rescue operation was put into effect by St. Augustine's governor, Francisco de Córcoles y Martinez, a strict military veteran. He was immediately concerned to prevent the presidio's citizens from leaving St. Augustine without a permit because he feared they would be treasure hunters, disrupting the formal salvage operations. All who owned a vessel, from a piroque to a sloop, were to bring it to the guardhouse under threat of fine or imprisonment. His own resources were limited to a two-masted sloop and piroques—canoes similar to the flat-bottom canoe used by Native Americans. He should have had two such sloops, but one had rotted and the other needed to be calked to make it seaworthy, so there was delay. Additionally, food supplies were short, but it was decided that the emergency demanded that food be sent to the fleet's survivors. The watchtower at Matanzas was put on alert to stop treasure hunters. It was assumed the treasure would be sent to St. Augustine as the treacherous weather made immediate shipment back to Havana untrustworthy. Much treasure was soon salvaged by Indian divers in the murky cold water. Salvaging had become a routine operation for the Spaniards, who were developing an apparatus to aid the divers.

When word of the disaster reached pirate ears, great haste was made to reach the Florida coast, using the Bahamas as a base. Jamaica's governor, Archibald Hamilton, tried to get Royal Navy ships involved, but the commanders refused. He then purchased shares in privateers he had commissioned, and Captain Henry Jennings promised to provide him with plunder. Jennings hired fourteen black and white divers and was soon disbursing Spanish salvage operations on the Florida coast. He first acted like a pirate in early 1716, when with three vessels and 150–300 men, his fleet ambushed the Spanish salvage camp. After forcing the retreat of 40 soldiers from the site, Jennings completed his operations and sailed back to Jamaica with an estimated 350,000 pesos. Still, most of the treasure arrived in Havana or St. Augustine.

Woodes Rogers destroys the Pirate Republic

The Bahamian Pirate Republic would fall, but not from the Spanish efforts; rather it would collapse from within as Britain at last established its authority over the islands. In January 1718, Woodes Rogers, designated captain general and governor of the Bahamas, announced that the king's pardon would be available to all pirates that took it by September 5. He prepared an expedition of 100 soldiers, 130 settlers, crews, supplies and religious pamphlets to clear the Bahamas of pirates. Accompanied by the Royal Navy, his fleet arrived in New Providence on July 22, where we have seen that Vane was trapped and then escaped. The colony consisted of about 200 former pirates and 300 Spanish refugees, some who had escaped from St. Augustine. In addition to the king's pardon, Rogers organized a government and began rebuilding the islands' fortifications, which had fallen into ruin because it was difficult to get the locals to work on them. Rogers's Royal Navy vessels then left for New York. He sent ships to Havana to conciliate the Spanish governor, but they never arrived. As noted, ex-pirate Benjamin Hornigold was sent to take Vane but, after a long absence, they could not find him. Hornigold was then sent to recapture the ships he had sent to Havana, the crews of which had become pirates along the way. Hornigold returned with ten prisoners, nine of whom Rogers executed in December. After this, while the pirates still sought to overthrow Rogers, they got no support.

Between the years 1718–21, a formal British administrative and military presence was centered on Nassau. Rogers's motto was "Piracy expelled, commerce restored." However, when he outfitted privateers in New Providence to go against places like St. Augustine, once they had embarked, their crews rose up against their captain, and they still became pirates. Thus, his efforts to destroy piracy sometimes failed. Woodes Rogers, the man caught in these contradictions, was born in Poole, Dorset, in 1679. His father moved the family to the great seaport of Bristol, where he was a successful merchant captain, owning shares in many ships, some involved in the slave trade. Woodes was apprenticed to a Bristol mariner to learn the trade of a sailor at the late age of eighteen. Such a position assured that he would be known in the Bristol seafaring community and given the privileges of a freeman. He completed his apprenticeship by 1704 and married Sarah Whetstone, the daughter of the influential rear admiral Sir William Whetstone. When his father died in 1706, he inherited his business.

During the War of the Spanish Succession, Bristol ships, including four owned by Rogers, were given letters of marque to strike at enemy shipping. Rogers turned to privateering to recoup loses caused by French privateers. In 1707, Rogers approached William Dampier, a navigator and friend of his father's, to participate in an ambitious privateering expedition against the Spaniards in the Pacific. His voyage would last from 1708 to 1711. In going from the Atlantic to the Pacific Ocean, Rogers avoided the dangerous Drake Passage, going farther south to open water, but very close to Antarctica. Rogers stocked his ship with limes to fend off scurvy. In 1709, he attacked Guayaquil, Ecuador, and negotiated a modest ransom. Finally the expedition captured a large Spanish vessel off the west coast of Mexico and limped home by way of Guam, which welcomed the two privateers despite being a Spanish island. Upon returning home, Rogers and his partners were promptly imprisoned for breaching the East India Company's monopoly of the Pacific. His investors were able to double their money; Rogers, however, got little. Still, his exploits made him a national hero.

To perpetuate his fame and pay his debts, he wrote a book titled *A Cruising Voyage Around the World*. In it, he saw the French rather than pirates or Spanish privateers as Britain's chief enemy in the War of the Spanish Succession. He felt that Britain had a superior navy and superior goods compared to both France and Spain, and yet, did not get its share of the West Indies trade. Even Spanish merchants were attracted to British goods. France, as an ally of Spain, had infiltrated the Spanish flota system and dominated trade at the designated port of Cadiz. On the basis of its superior navy and goods, Britain had the right to seize any Spanish-claimed American land it wanted.

At home in Bristol, Rogers's financial position continued to decline. His influential father-in-law died, he had to sell his home and his crew sued him over distribution of the Pacific spoils. He was forced into bankruptcy. To get out of the red, he decided to lead another expedition, this time against pirates. In 1713, he sailed toward the Indian Ocean and the notorious pirate island of Madagascar, which he scouted for future forays. A year later, he made friends with George I, who admired him, and he agreed that Rogers's company could manage the Bahamas in exchange for a share of the colony's profits. The proprietors of Carolina would lease the Bahamas to Rogers's company for twenty-one years, and that is how Rogers came to enter New Providence harbor as governor in 1718.

A year later, Rogers learned that Spain and Britain were at war again, while two-timing France was an ally of Britain. In May 1719, Spaniards sent an invasion fleet toward Nassau, but the city was saved when the Spanish fleet changed its destination to Pensacola, which the French had just captured. Less than a year later, the Spanish authorities renewed their enterprise and arrived before Nassau. By this time, British commitment to the Bahamas was evident, as Woodes Rogers had improved Nassau's defenses. To avoid the forts, Spanish troops landed on Hog Island, which sheltered the city's harbor. Rogers used local militia to drive them off, the first time a Spanish attack had been blunted.

The Bahamas Pirate "Republic"

Rogers continued work on the fortifications and bought supplies using his own credit, on the hope that he would be reimbursed by his investors in Bristol. However, his merchant backers refused to give him further credit, and he became overextended financially. His health began to suffer, and he spent six weeks in Charles Town, South Carolina. In 1721, he decided to return to Britain but on arrival found that his company had been liquidated and that a new governor had been appointed for the Bahamas. To further his indignity, he was imprisoned for debt.

Rogers was released from prison only when his creditors took pity on him and absolved him from debts. Around 1722, he was approached by a "Captain Charles Johnson" who wanted to use his knowledge to help him create a best-selling history of pirates. The book made Rogers famous, although he was by no means a pirate. George I granted him a pension, and in 1728, George II named him again the governor of the Bahamas.

While he had been able to turn back the Spanish, he experienced the difficulties of most colonial governors. He could not get his newly created

Woodes Rogers, governor of the Bahamas (on right), being presented with the plans to the port of Nassau by his son. Painting by William Hogarth, 1729. *Courtesy of Wikimedia Commons.*

assembly to vote in favor of taxes to maintain the vital fortifications. He dissolved it and was exhausted by the political conflict, so that he again went to Charles Town for his health in early 1731. He returned the next year to the Bahamas, but never regained his strength and died in Nassau on July 15, 1732.

Thus for a while St. Augustine came to be protected from Bahamian pirate raids by the offspring of a Bristol merchant family, who as governor, dispersed the pirates and brought a measure of stability to the Bahamas. This did not mean that the British government would become cooperative with St. Augustine. In 1745, the situado fleet coming out of Havana with supplies and coinage consisted of two small galleons, a frigate and a brigantine. When they left Havana, a violent storm separated one of the galleons, which was carrying 47,000 pesos, from the rest. This disabled vessel was forced to take refuge in an inlet of the Bahamas. The crew voted to repair their ship and continue on to St. Augustine. However, before they were able to get a favorable wind to carry their vessel out of the inlet, a British frigate with six cannon and twenty-nine men found them, threw out grappling hooks and took them. The British towed their prize to Providence Island, where the supplies and money on board were confiscated, although the crew was released and made it back to Cuba. This was a great blow to St. Augustine, which had not received the situado for several years, and the resulting promise from Cuba that it would be replaced was hollow, for it would take years. The Bahamas continued to be a danger for Spanish ships bound for St. Augustine.

Chapter Six
St. Augustine Takes on the Carolinas

In 1670, Charles II of England gave the territory of Carolina to eight friends in appreciation of their services in restoring him to the throne. Known as the Lord Proprietors, they also held the Bahamas, but began bestowing grants of land in the northern limits of Spanish Florida. These Lord Proprietors would govern Carolina until it was bought out by the crown in 1729, when the area became the royal colonies of South and North Carolina.

PORT ROYAL

In 1680, Henry, Lord Cardross, migrated to Carolina and set up a colony at Port Royal, South Carolina. Born in 1650, the son of a noble Scottish family, he was imprisoned at the age of twenty-five after opposing the Anglican leanings of the administration in Scotland. At Port Royal, he built Stuart Town for his settlers, and with its superb harbor, it seemed it would outstrip the other settlement at Charles Town as the capital of Carolina. In 1684, he brought a ship carrying ten Scottish Covenanter (firm Presbyterian) families who had rebelled against the policies of the established Scottish Church.

Of course, Spain also claimed the Carolina coast, and thus the Cardross's Port Royal colony was seen as an infringement. In Havana and St. Augustine, a decree announced that no English colonists would be allowed to reside below Charles Town. It also noted that Grammont had used Charles Town as a base. In July 1686, privateer captain Alejandro Tomas de León sailed out

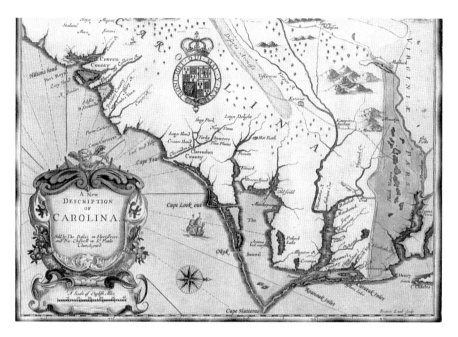

Engraving of "A New Description of Carolina," drawn by John Speed and engraved by Francis Lamb, 1676. *Courtesy of Wikimedia Commons.*

of Havana and refreshed his fleet at St. Augustine, taking on 153 garrison troops, Indians and the newly formed black militia. Three months earlier, he had captured one of Grammont's oared galliots, perhaps postponing his attack on St. Augustine.

At Stuart Town, Cardross was away in Britain, and the Spaniards attacked his empty colony, laying it to waste. Following the refugees from Stuart Town, León also came upon South Carolina governor Landgrave Morton's plantation and that of his provincial secretary on Edisto Island. The Spaniards freed enslaved Christian Indians and carried away thirteen African slaves. Morton's brother-in-law was killed. They looted and burned plantations, activities that went far beyond their original orders but made perfect sense to a privateer.

Then the Spanish privateers moved north to take Charles Town. Unfortunately for the Spaniards, a storm intervened, scattering Captain de Leon's fleet. His ship became lost and sank at sea, and the captain drowned. The remaining ships returned to St. Augustine.

A Slave Colony

In 1708, South Carolina's governor, Nathaniel Johnson, reported that black slaves were now a majority, numbering 4,100. In contrast, Indian slaves numbered only 1,400 and whites, 4,080. The colony had become a society of wealthy planters and merchants, with a poor middle class of indentured servants, with the majority of the population and wealth being in black slaves. They had come from several sources. Grammont had sold slaves captured from Campeche at Charles Town. Some of Charles Town's black slaves were sailors on slaving ships who had been promised freedom when they returned from a voyage.

To the ire of Carolinians, when their slaves ran away, they fled to St. Augustine, where Spanish authorities offered them refuge rather than returning them to their masters. This policy had developed from 1687, after the pirate raids and just four years after the creation of St. Augustine's pardo and moreno militia. At St. Augustine, the Carolina runaways took notice of the numerous free blacks and mulattos already in the city. Many Carolina

Watercolor of The Old Plantation, attributed to John Rose, circa 1785–90. *Courtesy of Abby Aldrich Rockefeller Folk Art Museum.*

blacks seemed to know Catholicism and also asked for religious sanctuary, a plea that no Spanish governor could turn down.

Governor Diego de Quiroga offered the runaways temporary sanctuary, while he consulted with Spanish authorities on how to treat them. The men earned wages as ironsmiths and laborers on the Castillo, and the women did the same as domestics. All were instructed in Catholic doctrine, baptized and married in the church. When Carolina sent an agent to get the slaves back, Quiroga refused to send them, instead offering to purchase them from their owners. This was abandoned by 1733, however, as Carolinians took advantage of the practice, demanding high prices for their runaway slaves.

Groups of escaped slaves continued to flee to St. Augustine. Finally in 1693, Charles II made slave sanctuary in St. Augustine an official policy on the basis of religious and humanitarian concerns. From then on, Carolinians not only felt the sting of losing their labor force but also feared that the Spaniards were promoting runaways and were behind slave uprisings.

Pirates Defend Against the Franco-Spanish Attack

As they tried to promote peace, the English Proprietors of Carolina washed their hands of the rivalry between Charles Town and St. Augustine, blaming the Carolinians because they had "received the pirates and privateers that have unjustly burnt and robbed the houses of the Spaniards." The proprietors pointed out that from 1689, Spain and England were actually European allies in the effort to head off Louis XIV's expanding France. Still, Charles Town maintained a lively trade in rice with the Bahamas, where its merchants were invariably caught up in pirate forays that ignored the constraints of diplomacy.

News of the outbreak of the War of the Spanish Succession was welcomed in Carolina in mid-1702; its officials acted immediately. South Carolina Governor James Moore, a slave trader, was so exalted by the possibility of profit that in December of 1702, he decided to lead an expedition to besiege St. Augustine. His force included pirates like Colonel Robert Daniel, who had participated in the pillage of Vera Cruz. When Daniel's vanguard arrived at St. Augustine, he promptly sacked the town. Moore, who arrived soon after, failed to besiege the Castillo, and he and his captains would be accused of having kept a large share of the town's plunder rather than distributing it equally in shares—a hallmark of pirates and privateers. Angry at his failure at St. Augustine, Moore would launch a series of raids against the weakly defended Spanish-Indian settlements of northern Florida, where he gained great success.

While the 1686 expedition against Carolina had failed because of the elements and the Carolina invasion of 1702 had been foiled, St. Augustine's authorities still harbored desires to destroy Charles Town. The idea of a combined Franco-Spanish expedition from St. Augustine against Charles Town first arose in 1704, when St. Augustine's governor, Joseph Zúniga y Cerda, discussed the plan as a means of revenge for Moore's attack. French Captain Pierre Le Moyne d'Iberville, an experienced privateer, had a grandiose plan for assaulting Carolina. He wanted a French fleet to join with a Spanish fleet at Havana, which would then descend on Charles Town. The expedition was to be paid for by holding other Carolina communities hostage after destroying Charles Town. It was not until late 1705 that Iberville secured permission from France for the purpose. The king provided ships and some troops but required Iberville to bear the upfront cost of outfitting the expedition.

Iberville left France in January 1706 with a fleet of twelve ships carrying 600 French troops. They first sailed for the West Indies, where pirates were recruited at Martinique, and they contributed to Iberville's successful siege

Pierre Le Moyne d'Iberville, circa 1700. *From "The Sun King, Louis XIV and The New World," an exhibition organized by the Louisiana State Museum between 1984–85.*

of English-held Nevis. Iberville then released part of his squadron and sailed for Havana. There, he attempted to interest Spanish authorities in supporting his expedition against Charles Town but with limited success, due in part to a raging yellow fever epidemic in the city. It decimated the expedition's possible troops, and Iberville himself succumbed to it. Before he died, he handed control of the expedition to Captain Jacques Lefebvre.

Determined, Lefebvre sailed from Havana with five ships, carrying about 300 French soldiers under the command of General Arbousset and 200 Spanish volunteers led by General Esteban de Berroa, who had commanded the force that raised the siege of St. Augustine in 1702. The fleet first made for St. Augustine, where the governor, Francisco de Córcoles y Martínez, outfitted the expedition with more volunteers, thirty infantry and about fifty "Christian" Indians.

The combined fleet sailed from St. Augustine on August 31. While en route to Charles Town, a sloop was spotted, and the French warship *Brillant* gave chase, only to be separated from the rest of the squadron. The sloop was an English privateer sent out by Governor Johnson to intercept Spanish supply ships; it reported the fleet's movement toward Charles Town.

Pirates Defend Charles Town

Charles Town and its countryside were also suffering the ravages of yellow fever, when the news of the Spanish fleet arrived. In response, Governor Johnson called out the militia. Of South Carolina's white population, an estimated 900 men served in the militia. Anticipating that a landing would be attempted on James Island, which guarded the southern approach to Charles Town's harbor, Johnson posted the militia there under the command of another slave trader, Lieutenant Colonel William Rhett. The northern point of James Island was fortified by Fort Johnson, which housed a few token cannon. The militia also improvised a flotilla, which included former pirates. Rhett had moved to Carolina in 1698. He soon became a successful leader, completing a new mansion and acquiring a sugar plantation. Although he led Carolina's pirates against the invaders, he would eventually become a pirate hunter.

The Franco-Spanish fleet arrived off the harbor bar on September 4, 1706. Despite the absence of the *Brillant* (which carried much of the French force, including the campaign's guns, shovels, spades, shells and General Arbousset), Captain Lefebvre and his fleet crossed the bar on September 7,

Colonel William Rhett House, built circa 1712–20, in Charleston, SC. *Courtesy of Wikimedia Commons.*

View of Charles Town by Thomas Leitch, circa 1773. *Courtesy of Museum of Early Southern Decorative Arts.*

and delivered an ultimatum the next day. In pirate fashion, he demanded a ransom of 50,000 pesos, threatening to destroy Charles Town if it was not paid. Governor Johnson dismissed the demand, claiming the town was worth 40 million pesos.

On September 9, the invaders landed two separate forces. One force of 160 men plundered plantations near the Charles Town neck, but the force was recalled when Governor Johnson sent militia out in boats to oppose them. A second party landed on James Island but was also driven away by the threat of opposition. Late that night, Johnson received word that the neck was occupied by the enemy and sent Rhett with 100 men to investigate. Arriving at daybreak the next day, they surprised the invaders, who fled after a brief skirmish in which 12 were killed and about 60 captured.

Two days later, Rhett sailed out and found the enemy had left. His fleet was manned by local pirates, enlisted by South Carolina authorities in the defense of Charles Town. Finally the lost *Brillant* appeared. Its captain had misjudged the distance from St. Augustine and arrived farther north before turning around. General Arbousset landed his troops east of Charles Town, but the *Brillant* was surrounded by Rhett's fleet; Arbousset and his men surrendered after suffering as many as thirty killed. The prisoners included ninety to one hundred Indians; most of these were sold as slaves. Carolina officials declared October 17 a day of thanksgiving for the successful defense of Charles Town.

STEDE BONNET'S CAREER

Although they came to view piracy as a threat to stability and trade, nearly a decade later, Charles Town's leaders tolerated pirates out of necessity. This was the time when Woodes Rogers would push the pirates out of the Bahamas, and his example was not lost on Charles Town's merchants and planters. In the case of pirates like Stede Bonnet of Barbados, he would find Carolina to be a hostile environment. An educated and wealthy gentleman, when Bonnet began pirating in 1717, he had no knowledge of seafaring. Still, he moved ahead and bought a sixty-ton sloop, the *Revenge*, equipping it with six guns. Not only did Bonnet buy his ship, but he paid his crew wages rather than offering shares of plunder, and he was able to enlist a crew of more than seventy men, which included many blacks. For sailing, he relied on his quartermaster and officers and, as a result, his influence over the crew fluctuated. He said that when he tired of the life of a pirate, as he inevitably did, he would retire to Spain or Portugal, where his reputation would be unknown.

Bonnet's initial cruise took him from Barbados to the Carolinas, Virginia and New York. First, he went to the Virginia coast at the entrance to

St. Augustine Takes on the Carolinas

Chesapeake Bay, where he captured and plundered four vessels and burned the Barbadian ship *Turbet* to keep news of his crimes from spreading. He then sailed north toward New York City, taking two more ships. He also landed to obtain supplies and release his captives on Gardiners Island, a sanctuary at the west end of Long Island. By August 1717, Bonnet had returned to the Carolinas, where he lay outside of Charles Town Harbor waiting for prey. He caught two more ships, a brigantine from Boston and a Barbadian sloop. He stripped the brigantine but brought the cargo-filled Barbadian sloop to an inlet on the North Carolina coast. From there, Bonnet set course for the pirate republic in the Bahamas. On the way, he encountered and escaped from a Spanish man-of-war. However, the *Revenge* was badly damaged, he was seriously wounded and half the crew of the sloop was lost. Putting into Nassau, Bonnet recruited new men, refitted the *Revenge* and increased its armament to twelve guns. Later records show the crew were a mixed lot, most of whom originated from port cities like London and Bristol, Glasgow, Aberdeen and Dublin. Some blacks came from Jamaica, Charles Town or Bath in the Carolinas, and others were Dutch and Portuguese. Such was the multi-ethnic character of what would be his last crew.

At Nassau, Bonnet met the infamous pirate Blackbeard, who teamed with him. As Bonnet was unpopular with his crew, Teach quickly took over command of the *Revenge*. They went to the North Carolina coast where Blackbeard cleverly beached the majority of his crew, robbed the *Revenge* and two other vessels of their supplies and sailed away for parts unknown aboard the sloop *Adventure*, carrying his loot. Double-crossed, Bonnet searched for Blackbeard but never found him.

In North Carolina, Bonnet took the king's pardon and hoped to gain a letter of marque, but the temptation to renew his piracy was too strong. He tried to disguise his return to piracy by engaging in a pretense of trade with the next two vessels he attacked. Soon afterward, however, Bonnet quit the charade.

In July 1718, the *Revenge* cruised north to Delaware Bay, pillaging another eleven vessels, most of which were coming from or to Philadelphia. The best of them was a sixty-ton sloop bound from Antigua to Philadelphia carrying a cargo of rum, molasses, sugar cotton and indigo. While Bonnet freed many of his prizes after looting them, he retained control of the last two ships he captured: the sloops *Francis* and *Fortune*. When the month ended, he renamed the *Revenge* the *Royal James*, and with the two captured sloops, sailed southward from Delaware Bay. Disregarding his early pay policy, Bonnet and his crew divided their loot into £10 shares and distributed them amongst themselves. Word of his depredations on the Delaware spread to Charles Town.

BONNET VERSUS RHETT AND TROTT

Late in August, news reached Charles Town that Bonnet's vessels were nearby, moored in the Cape Fear River to the north, where he was careening and repairing the *Royal James*. South Carolina's governor, Robert Johnson, authorized Colonel William Rhett, the successful defender of Charles Town in 1706, to lead a naval expedition against the pirates and after chasing some, Rhett arrived at the mouth of the Cape Fear River, North Carolina on September 26, 1718 with two 8-gun sloops and 130 men. Bonnet initially mistook Rhett's squadron for merchantmen and sent only three periaguas to capture them. Unfortunately for Rhett, his pilot ran his flagship *Henry* and the other sloop aground at the river mouth, enabling Bonnet's canoe crews to approach, recognize the hostile armed sloops and return to warn Bonnet. That night, the rising tide lifted the sloops off the river bottom.

Bonnet's crew were scattered among his three vessels. During the night, Bonnet brought them aboard the *Royal James* and planned for a running fight in the morning rather than risk the Cape Fear River's narrow channels in the dark. At daybreak, Bonnet set sail toward Rhett and the two South Carolinian sloops split up in an effort to trap the pirates. Bonnet tried to avoid the trap by steering the *Royal James* close to the river's western shore, but he ran aground. Rhett's closing sloops also ran aground, leaving only the *Henry* within pistol shot of the *Royal James*.

The confrontation was at a stalemate, with the participants immobilized in the shallows. Bonnet's men had the advantage because their deck was heeled away from their adversaries, while the *Henry*'s deck was tilted toward the pirates, exposing Rhett's men to musket fire. Bonnet's force suffered twelve casualties while killing ten and wounding fourteen of Rhett's crew. Most of Bonnet's crew fought enthusiastically, challenging their enemies to board and fight hand to hand in pirate style. Bonnet patrolled the deck with a pistol drawn; a few of the Carolina prisoners who had been forced to join the pirate crew refused to fire on Rhett's men.

The battle was ultimately decided when the rising tide lifted Rhett's sloops free, while temporarily leaving the *Royal James* stranded. Bonnet was left helpless, watching while Rhett's vessels repaired their rigging and closed to board his vessel. Outnumbered almost three to one, Bonnet ordered his gunner to blow up the *Royal James*'s powder magazine. He attempted this but was overruled by the remainder of the crew, who surrendered. Rhett arrested them as pirates and returned to Charles Town with his prisoners.

In Charles Town, Bonnet was separated from the bulk of his crew and held in the provost marshal's house along with his boatswain and sailing master. On October 24, Bonnet and his sailing master escaped by colluding with local merchant Richard Tookerman, who had ties to pirates in the Bahamas. Governor Johnson placed a £700 bounty on Bonnet's head and dispatched teams to track him down. Bonnet and the sailing master, accompanied by a slave and an Indian, obtained a boat and made for the north shore of Charles Town Harbor, but contrary winds and lack of supplies forced them onto Sullivan's Island. Governor Johnson sent a force under Rhett to Sullivan's Island to hunt for Bonnet. They discovered the escapees, killing the sailing master and wounding the slaves but sparing Bonnet. He was returned to Charles Town, and while he awaited trial, a mob threatened the court of guard in an attempt to free the remaining pirates, an event the authorities feared had been caused by the lack of a speedy trial.

On November 10, 1718, Bonnet was brought to trial before vice-admiralty judge and Rhett's brother-in-law Nicholas Trott, who would later marry his widow. Trott was also nephew of Sir Nicholas Trott, the governor of the Bahamas who had tangled with pirates. The Trott, Rhett and Richard Shelton families were closely tied together in the slave trade, supporting the proprietors of Carolina in colonial assembly and pushing the hope that Anglicanism would become the established church of South Carolina. By the time of Trott's appointment as vice-admiralty judge in 1716, he and Rhett controlled virtually all of royal and proprietary offices in South Carolina.

Trott had already sat in judgment on Bonnet's crew and sentenced most of them to hang. Bonnet was formally charged with only two acts of piracy—his Delaware activities against the *Francis* and the *Fortune*, whose commanders were on hand to testify against him. His boatswain had turned king's evidence in the trial of Bonnet's crew and now also testified against Bonnet. Along with most of his crew, Bonnet pled not guilty and conducted his own defense without assistance of counsel, cross-examining the witnesses. Two days later, Trott presented a sermon to Bonnet, in which he emphasized that he had been damned by God for his unholy behavior, calling into question his credentials as a gentleman and concluding by sentencing him to death.

A day later, twenty-two men of Bonnet's crew, who had already been tried, were hanged at West Point near Charles Town. While a remainder awaited

Engraving of the hanging of Stede Bonnet in 1719. *From Charles Johnson's* A General History of Pirates. *Courtesy of Wikimedia Commons.*

execution, including Bonnet, the gentleman pirate wrote to Governor Johnson, begging for clemency and promising to have his arms and legs cut off as assurance that he would never again commit piracy. Johnson noted that Bonnet's visibly disintegrating mind moved many Carolinians to pity, particularly the female population, and London papers later reported that the governor delayed his execution seven times. However, Bonnet was hanged in Charles Town on December 10, 1718.

Charles Town's merchants and planters were finding pirates more dangerous than helpful. Those who threatened their trade and political relationships ended up as Bonnet and his crew did.

Chapter Seven

𝕳avana 𝕾upports 𝕾t. 𝕬ugustine

Until the 1730s, Havana, Cuba was almost the only immediate source of supply and troops for St. Augustine. In 1702, Havana sent a relief force, blocking St. Augustine's harbor and landing troops on Anastasia Island to raise Governor Moore's siege of the presidio. In 1740, another Cuban relief force made General Oglethorpe abandon his siege of the Castillo. St. Augustine's needs focused on the great port of Havana. It was located on the northern coast of Cuba, within easy navigation of Florida.

In its early years, Havana's history was much like that of St. Augustine. The trading port was first burned and plundered by a French pirate in 1555. However, that pirate left without obtaining the enormous wealth of a flota, which had not arrived in the city. As with St. Augustine, these attacks prompted the Spanish crown to fund the construction of the first fortresses to not only counteract the pirates and enemies but also exert more regulation over commerce with the West Indies and to limit the extensive smuggling that had increased due to the trade restrictions imposed by the Casa de Contratación in Seville.

Following a 1561 royal decree, all ships in the flota headed for Spain were required to assemble in the Havana Bay. Vessels arrived from May through August, waiting for the best weather conditions, and then the fleet departed Havana to reach Spain by September. This boosted the commerce of Havana, which involved precious metals, alpaca wool, emeralds, leather, mahoganies, spices, dye sticks, corn, cassava and cocoa. These ships also fueled Havana's agriculture and manufactures, since the fleets had to be supplied with food, water and other products needed for the Atlantic voyage. In 1563, the captain

Depiction of seventeenth-century Havana. *Courtesy of Wikimedia Commons.*

general of Cuba moved his residence to Havana from the rival port Santiago de Cuba, thus sanctioning its status as capital of Cuba. Almost thirty years later, Philip II of Spain granted Havana the title of city. While Havana grew to support St. Augustine, much of Cuba's long coast was open to pirates, who sought its cays, innumerable small islands that made an ideal base.

Reform in Spanish Naval Affairs and Trade

Havana became a crucial base for the emerging Spanish Royal Navy, which came into its own in the eighteenth century. The use of galley fleets finally ended in 1748 with the conclusion of the War of Jenkins's Ear, although merchants and raiders still used them. Replacing them required a new type of warship, a feat accomplished by Admiral Antonio Gaztaneta. Born in 1656 in the Basque region of Spain, he served as the king's shipbuilder in 1715 and superintendent general of the shipyards in Cantabria. He designed sleeker and more seaworthy ships as well standardizing the naval ships to

be rated consistently by the number of guns they carried. It was he who first saw the advantage of the Havana shipyard as an extension to those being developed in Spain.

Trade with the West Indies was also changing. By 1680, sand bars and silting had made Seville's Guadalquivir River impassible to large ships and forced the Spanish government to transfer the Indies monopoly from Seville to Cadiz, which had a broad bay that provided immediate access to the Atlantic. In the eighteenth century, Cadiz experienced a golden age in which three-quarters of all Spanish trade with the

Jose Antonio de Guztaneta, an 1847 copy of the original by Landsberghs. *Courtesy of Wikimedia Commons.*

Americas left from its port, with its own arsenal and ship outfitting facilities. Even in 1765, when the city lost its monopoly of trade with the Indies, its trade would remain brisk. It became one of Spain's most cosmopolitan cities and home of merchant communities from various countries, including rich French and Irish families.

Another change was described by Woodes Rogers, who claimed that the Spanish monopoly of Indies trade was no longer in effect as: "Our English manufactures were annually shipped off in their galleons, either in the name of Spanish factors, or sold at Cadiz to the Spanish merchants, who sent them to the Indies on their own accounts." This was legal trade and was supplemented by smuggling "not only with merchants, but [also] with" the Spanish patrolling guarda costas. Drake would have been astounded; the prime English effort was now to sell manufactured goods in Cadiz.

Defense of Cadiz against the English (1625) by Francisco Zurbaran, 1634. Using galleys, the Spaniards were successful in beating off the expedition planned by the Duke of Buckingham, making up for Drake's devastating attack in 1587. *Courtesy Museo del Prado, Madrid.*

In 1728, the crown and Cantabrian merchants would begin to dilute Cadiz's trade monopoly. That year Philip V established the Real Compañía Guipuzcoana de Caracas in the privateer center of San Sebastian, giving its merchants a monopoly over Venezuela's trade. The company's establishment was viewed as a reforming measure, and it boosted commerce with the Americas. It was still a monopoly, but it foreshadowed a loosening of restrictions as more companies were formed. In 1740, Havana would form its own Royal Company. That same year, the fleet and galleon system was abandoned, although it was resurrected for New Spain fourteen years later, showing that the organizations that profited from the system continued to support it. Still, Spanish policy opened the trade of Spanish and American ports as never before, making the traditional flotas unnecessary.

Havana Prospers with Reform

As a result of Spain's trade and naval reforms in the late seventeenth and eighteenth centuries, Havana grew and prospered. At first tobacco was the dominant export, but by the mid-eighteenth century, sugar and hides had overtaken it. In exchange, the port at Cadiz sent back oil, wine and European manufactured goods.

In 1674, the city walls were started as part of the same fortification effort that St. Augustine experienced. They would be completed by 1740. When they were taken as prisoners, even pirates contributed to the labor force. In the mid-eighteenth century, Havana had a garrison of 1,500 to 2,000 regulars from Spain and 2,457 to 6,342 white, pardo and moreno militia. Though poorly armed, the militia provided the superior troops because they were natives, largely immune to the diseases so prevalent in the Caribbean. In contrast, the regulars were constantly expiring from disease, costing three times as much to maintain in Cuba as they would have in Spain.

Similar to the Italian maritime republic of Venice, Havana had the most important Royal Ship Yard in the Indies. In 1713, the yard produced twelve ships-of-the-line of fifty-six guns for the Spanish fleet. The use of Cuban cedar, which did not splinter when hit by cannon balls and was cheaper and more durable than Spanish oak, gave the island a shipbuilding industry. The surrounding forests were regulated so that they would not be over cut. Logs were then sent down Cuban streams to the coast and shipped by boat to Havana. The yard became the best place in the Caribbean to have a ship refitted.

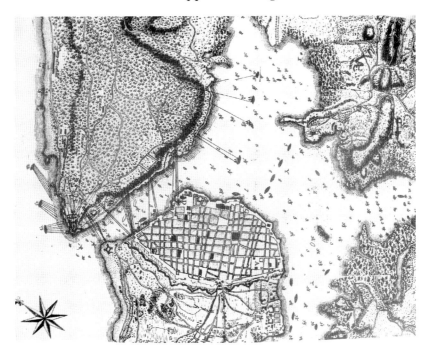

Map of Havana and environs by Thomas Mante, 1762. *Courtesy Naval Institute, Annapolis.*

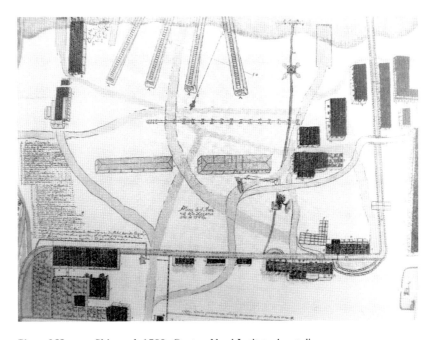

Plan of Havana Shipyard, 1788. *Courtesy Naval Institute, Annapolis.*

In 1741, Spanish minister Juan de Acosta gave crown support to Havana shipbuilding, ultimately making it the most productive yard in the Spanish Empire, surpassing even the shipyards in Cantabria. Havana still depended on Cantabria for iron, which was irregularly delivered. Before 1762, the Havana shipyard built forty-six ships for the navy, one as large as eighty guns. It also built fourteen smaller ships of twenty-four guns for raiding. The total was 40 percent of Spain's naval construction.

Cuban Privateers

The garrison fortress policy in both Havana and St. Augustine was defensive. However, in war time, such fixed fortifications would not be enough, for naval and privateer ships were also necessary if only to maintain connections between Havana and St. Augustine, let alone to attack the enemy. Like Britain and France, Spain needed to continue to encourage privateers to fill the naval gap. Cuban merchants supported privateering as a means of possible profit. They added a measure of private capital in support of governmental policies. By raiding and harassing British ships, they hoped to raise the cost of British merchants trying to do business in Cuba.

As early as 1638, Captain Diego Martin, alias Diego el Mulato, offered his services as a privateer to the Spanish authorities at Havana. He admired the king's support of the Catholic faith and agreed to protect the Cuban coast from Dutch and English pirates. The officials sent his request to Spain with the recommendation that he be pardoned from past indiscretions and offered a salary the equivalent of that of an admiral. Also in January 1684, a Spanish naval expedition from Havana was led by corsair Juan de Alarcón against the English privateering stronghold of Nassau. Alarcón stealthily approached Nassau with a commission issued by Havana's governor, José Fernández de Córdoba, and a pair of barcos luengos carrying two hundred men that was successful in destroying the town.

Support for St. Augustine

Normally, Florida's annual situado came from Mexico to Havana, where a portion was used to purchase food and necessities that were sent on to St. Augustine. Havana also monitored the British advancement from the Carolinas toward Florida. Havana and its Cuban hinterland provided militia, regulars, ships and food stocks for the defense of St. Augustine. Havana's harbor was ideal for privateers and guarda costas, regardless of the conditions of war and peace.

The need for Havana's support of St. Augustine is seen in the aftermath of Searles's raid in June 1668. Governor Francisco de la Guerra, facing a shortage of men, arms and food as a result of the raid, had the Havana frigate of Ignacio de Losa commandeered to bring corn to his starving city, as the ship was trading in the rich agricultural area of Apalache on the Gulf of Mexico. However, it was run aground before the task was completed. Guerra then asked the governor of Cuba to purchase "a frigate for St. Augustine," as well as canvas for the existing St. Augustine frigate whose sails had been stolen by the pirates. The new frigate's task would be to collect food in Florida for the presidio. Captain Antonio Menéndez Marqués carried the letter to Cuba on the only seaworthy vessel in St. Augustine, the pilot's launch. A small coastal ship, it could only make it to the Florida Keys, where a larger ship was hailed to carry Menéndez to Havana. On the return voyage from the Keys, the launch itself was run aground in a storm near St. Augustine, and the crew had to abandon it and walk home.

As yet Havana had no word of Searles's depredations. So Guerra had every scrap of canvas collected to make sails for the St. Augustine frigate. Guerra added a footnote to his original letter, emphasizing that he needed a "young St. Augustine-born armorer to replace the garrison's armorer, who had grown too old. Finally, on September 9, this frigate arrived in Havana Harbor—having taken more than three months to inform Havana of St. Augustine's dire situation. In Havana, Governor Dávila had the frigate's crew paid and the ship remasted, rigged and sent to Apalache to obtain corn. It was easier for him to outfit ships than it was to supply food, especially as Florida had the agriculturally productive Apalache area.

The 1702 siege had been raised by reinforcements from Havana. They were not, however, an unqualified success for St. Augustine's governor, Joseph Zúniga, who accused the Cuban General Esteban Berroa of incompetence. Zúniga hoped the Cuban rescue fleet would attack Moore's ships in the harbor and land troops to disrupt the siege. He, however, found it difficult to even communicate with Berroa, who gave every indication that he was in fact going to return to Havana. The Cuban claimed that he thought that Castillo had been taken by the English until Zúniga's adjutant came on board and set him straight. Berroa then landed his worst troops, raw Galician recruits, on Anastasia Island, and they proved to be too debilitated and inexperienced to proceed. In the meantime, Moore decided to burn his fleet and retreat back to Carolina by land. Berroa's men looted some of Moore's ships, but failed to share the spoils with the St. Augustine garrison. No effort was made to stop or pursue Moore and for this Zúniga blamed Berroa. Apparently, not all support from Havana was completely appreciated.

The Royal Havana Company

Following the spirit of reform, in 1740, the town council of Havana sent Martin de Aróstegui y Larrea, a rich merchant, to the court of Philip V, where he offered to provide the traditional amount of Cuban tobacco to Spain, and, on the return of his ships, would carry ammunition and food stuffs to Havana, which he would distribute to whites in the Florida presidios or for other uses designated by the crown. After deliberation, the crown accepted the offer.

Aróstegui returned from Spain in December 1740 with the news that the Spanish crown had created the Royal Company of Havana. It was established as a joint stock enterprise similar to the British East India Company. Philip V was among those who purchased stock in the company. The company was made up of Cuban entrepreneurs (chiefly Basques)

Tobacco-shredding machine attributed to Alonso Francisco Gonzalez. *Courtesy Archivo General de Indias, Seville.*

involved in the export of sugar and tobacco, the slave trade and shipbuilding. The Company was a sign that Havana had an emerging middle class.

Born in Aranas, Navarre, Aróstegui was named first president of the Royal Company of Havana. He was alguacil mayor of the Havana Inquisition, first president of the Royal Tobacco Factory and a knight of the Order of Santiago. He owned tobacco factories near Havana and built a substantial house in the city in 1759.

Unfortunately, Aróstegui actually concentrated on trading slaves and selling tobacco for his own personal gain to the British American colonies rather than supplying goods to Spain or St. Augustine. He was also in trouble with Spanish authorities over the cost of building ships in Havana's Royal Shipyard. In October 1749, Aróstegui wrote to Ferdinand VI's minister of state, José de Carvajal y Lancáster, about the cost of naval shipbuilding at Royal Shipyard for the Spanish crown. He defended himself against charges of mismanaging naval construction through overspending and excessive employment of workers. He argued that the quality of the Havana ships *Rayo* and the *Fenix*, both launched earlier in 1749, was superior. These two ships saw exemplary service in the Spanish navy, most notably the *Rayo*, which was still able to fight at the battle of Trafalgar in 1805. While the costs of naval construction at Havana were greater than expected, and the crown was anxious to bring the construction under state control, the claim of superior quality offset this. Moreover, when Aróstegui's business partners learned of his deeds in 1752, he was arrested and removed from the company.

Following Aróstegui's offer to the crown, the Royal Company was committed to supplying and populating Florida. It would replace the often late Mexican situado contract. A Royal Company agent and the governor of St. Augustine drew up a contract to provide the situado of supplies and specie for St. Augustine.

The Royal Company, however, did not have the resources to carry out these duties alone. It owned armed vessels, but it did not use them in risky privateering ventures. The company did not offer Florida farmers a price competitive to English merchants in the Carolinas, and St. Augustine still remained dependent on food imports as the company's contract continued until 1763. Gradually, the company would reduce its expenditures for Florida, meaning that it failed to adequately supply the presidios. It issued private contracts for ship construction and supplies of flour to feed St. Augustine. Some of the flour contracts went to New York City merchants who could best meet the demand.

Cubans in St. Augustine

By the eighteenth century, Cuba's population was almost evenly divided between whites, and blacks and mulattos. The former provided military, administrative and commercial services, while the latter provided the labor for the extensive fortifications, tobacco and sugar. Most black workers had originally been slaves, but as the seventeenth century progressed, half of them were freed.

With so many freed blacks and the continuing need for defense, Havana created black militia companies. These black companies first appeared in the 1570s, and by 1600, a one-hundred-man company was established. By 1667 two companies existed and by 1700 four companies. The companies were divided between free pardos and morenos, the former being mulatto militiamen, while the latter were blacks. Membership in the militia reinforced their status as freemen, gave them the right to bear arms and protected them from criminal prosecution in civil courts. As trained, veteran soldiers, these militiamen were recognized as valuable members of Cuban society.

When Menéndez initially settled St. Augustine, Havana officials actually conceived of Florida as a depository for unwanted black slaves. A century later, however, Governor Hita of St. Augustine actually requested that one hundred Havana recruits be sent to replace the Mexican recruits that he found incompetent. Cuban troops, chiefly pardos and morenos from Havana, joined St. Augustine's garrison in 1673, 1702 and 1709, and Governor Montiano used them to attack Georgia and South Carolina between 1742 and 1750. They were present in forays against St. Simons Island, Beaufort and Brunswick in the Cape Fear area.

Cuban pardos and morenos were not only successful soldiers, but they also married in St. Augustine and became part of the community. Joseph Cayertano Rivera was born in Campeche in 1712 and moved to Cuba before coming to St. Augustine in 1742 with reinforcements from Havana. Ten years later he was a soldier in Captain Álvaro López de Toledo's company of the garrison. In 1746, he married Catherine Hernández, a woman of little reputation as she was both a bastard child and of humble origins. In St. Augustine, pardos and morenos did not have wide latitude in their choice of a wife, but the possibility remained.

Other Cubans claimed to be of white lineage. The Pedrosa family of Havana asserted that they were related to Menéndez, the adelantado himself. The Ayala family of Havana was influential because of the exploits of Juan de Ayala Escobar. Born in Havana in 1635, he spent his youth as a sailor and privateer on merchant vessels in the Caribbean. In 1675, he married Magdelena de Uriza of Havana, the daughter of the adjutant of the Havana presidio, and began a military career. Through her father's influence, he was sent to Castillo de San Marcos in 1683 as a lieutenant and adjutant to the garrison. Magdelena returned to Havana with the children after only two years (she considered St. Augustine a backwater), but Juan remained and pursued his military career. In 1687 and again in 1702, he captained ships that sailed directly to Spain to ask for reinforcements at St. Augustine because of the failure of support from Havana and Vera Cruz. In the former year, he returned with eighty soldiers and a black slave, the first of what Ayala felt would be more. By 1703, he had

Soldiers, Havana blanco (on the right) and moreno militia battalions, 1764. St. Augustine's blancos and morenos may have had similar uniforms. *Courtesy Archivo General de Indias, Seville.*

become Sergeant Mayor of the garrison. In this position, he involved himself in securing precious provisions from Charles Town and sold them in his shop for high prices, essentially exploiting a population dependent on the situado for coin. In 1712, when Governor Francisco de Córcoles tried to arrest him for these illegal practices, the entire town threatened to rise up, forcing the governor to back down. After all, Ayala had relieved their hunger. From 1716 to 1718, Ayala served as interim governor. His successor, Antonio de Benavides, accused him of contraband trade, and he was imprisoned and sent to Cuba. There, in 1727, before his trial was dismissed, he died. While he experienced shame because his wife resided in Havana, he showed how popular a Cuban merchant-sailor could be in St. Augustine.

Havana and St. Augustine were tied by family relationships, by shipping that supplied St. Augustine and Florida and by the concern in Havana to use St. Augustine as a base to prevent British and French incursion. The Royal Company of Havana seemed to be an ideal reform to solve the situado delays. However, it was too commercially oriented and like its predecessor, it failed to supply the presidio on time.

Chapter Eight
The First Privateer War

The War of the Spanish Succession concluded in 1713 with the Peace of Utrecht and Philip Bourbon being recognized as King Philip V of Spain. He had renounced his place in the French line of succession, thereby precluding the union of the French and Spanish crowns, which had been feared in Britain and much of Europe. He retained Spain's overseas empire but ceded European territory to Austria and Savoy and gave Gibraltar and Minorca to Britain. He continued the Spanish crusade against the Turks and Barbary pirates in the Mediterranean.

The peace between Spain and Britain, however, lasted for only five years. In 1718, the War of the Quadruple Alliance broke out in Europe, with all the powers lining up against Spain because of its ambitions in Italy. In May, a force was prepared in Havana to attack the Bahamas, but while en route, it had to be diverted to retake Pensacola, which had just fallen to the French. Finally, a year later, a second Spanish fleet of three frigates, a brigantine and eight armed sloops appeared at the entrance to Nassau Harbor. As mentioned, Woodes Rogers had erected new fortifications, expelled pirates and now commanded the defense, so that the port was ready. When the Spanish fleet landed its troops away from the harbor at night, a pair of free black sentries fired on them. The Spanish mistook the two as an army and backed off. Nassau was saved, although Rogers was exhausted both financially and physically by the effort.

Philip V in Defense of the Sacrament of the Eucharist against a Turkish infidel, reminiscent of a Barbary pirate, early eighteenth century. This painting is by an unnamed artist and is painted in the Cuzco tradition. *Courtesy Stern/ Davis Collection.*

THE GUARDA COSTAS AND ST. AUGUSTINE'S PRIVATEERS

The Peace of Utrecht had also granted the British the asiento, the monopoly of non-Spanish slave trading in the Spanish colonies for thirty years, a grant that was passed on to the South Sea Company. The grant included the right for an annual ship to trade 500 tons of other goods. This gave British ships the opportunity to enter Spanish-American ports on many pretenses and carry on trade. The smuggling forced Spain to develop a means to patrol its colonial waters and search for violations, a policy that was recognized in 1729 by the Treaty of Seville, which confirmed the Spanish right to board and search British ships.

To prevent the smuggling fostered by the asiento, the Spanish governors licensed private ships to be guarda costas, which boarded foreign ships, confiscated them and imprisoned crews if they were found to be smuggling. Complaints by British merchants about the highhanded activities of guarda costas mounted in the 1720s. In fact, guarda costas operated as privateers with the advantage that they carried on their activities during peace. In April 1729, the governor of Cuba licensed a guarda costa, under Captain Félix de Hurtado. It was fitted out "in a warlike manner as a privateer," to protect the coast of Cuba. It was to prevent trade in prohibited goods and to capture pirates that infested the coast. Prizes were to be taken to Havana, where distribution of the proceeds was made between the captain, his crew and those who bore the cost of fitting out the ship. While the agreement was for a guarda costa, it would have been familiar to a privateer.

Under these conditions, St. Augustine was put on the alert. It should be remembered that during the War of the Spanish Succession, Governor Zúniga had two frigates and several piroques for his use. He had sent the frigates to Havana to seek reinforcements when word came of Moore's invasion of Florida. One of them, however, was caught on the St. Augustine bar as the enemy approached and had to be destroyed. The other, *La Gloria*, captained by Luis Alfonso, made it to Havana and managed to dispatch a relief fleet. The number of ships had not changed from 1715, when the treasure fleet was salvaged in St. Augustine.

To add to the garrison ships, Governor Antonio de Benavides issued letters of marque. In late April 1720, the first Spanish privateers with the governor's letters of marque appeared off the Virginia Capes. The legislature of South Carolina reported that their runaway slaves were making pitch and tar for Spanish vessels at St. Augustine, thus supporting privateer activities.

Havana also supported St. Augustine's privateer war against the British colonies by providing privateers, soldiers and sailors. In 1720, three Havana privateers were fitted out for raiding the British colonial coast. Off the Carolinas, a two-gun sloop with fifty men from Havana captured an eight-gun London ship and then a sloop from Glasgow.

Early in 1720, Alexander Spotswood, Governor of Virginia, described the position of St. Augustine and suggested—as the Carolinians had already attempted—that it be conquered. He claimed its strategic location on the Florida channel between Florida and the Bahamas had made it an objective for "any of our men of war or privateers that may be placed on that station." He would soon be aware of Spanish privateers as they appeared on the Virginia coast and committed depredations, which he thought he had snuffed out a few years before, when he had executed pirates like Edward Teach.

Spotswood reacted to the new threat to Virginia's trade, admitting, "privateers fitted out at St. Augustine have for the past month infested

Governor Alexander
Spotswood of Virginia
by Charles Bridges, 1736.
Courtesy State of Virginia.

this coast." He claimed they were violating the Limitations of Suspension of Arms, as Spain and Britain were now formally at peace, and thus the privateers were acting like pirates. By September, he was certain that the privateers had letters of marque from Governor Benavides. He sent a flag to St. Augustine, and Benavides claimed to be unaware of the truce when he authorized the privateers. Benavides was willing to return some of the captured prizes, but he would retain others. He was apparently unaware that the War of the Quadruple Alliance had ceased in Europe in 1720.

In 1721, Spotswood, in order to counteract the "resort of Bandittos" that St. Augustine had become, asked Britain's board of trade for protection in the form of two forty-five-gun man-of-wars and a sloop for shallow waters. Thus, one man-of-war could be careened while the other patrolled. He promised that if these ships were in place, there would no trading losses in coastal Virginia.

Despite the efforts of Governor Spotswood, Spanish privateers continued their efforts and chose their target wisely, as Chesapeake Bay was without guard ships at the time. Anyone who tried to leave Chesapeake or Delaware Bays could not avoid the Spanish privateers. On April 28, 1720, a St. Augustine sloop of four guns and seventy men captured a ship from London bound for South Carolina, followed by a sloop from New Jersey bound for North Carolina. With three French sailors as a prize crew, the captured sloop was to follow the privateer to St. Augustine. However, the prisoner mate fooled the French sailors on board, steering it in the opposite direction, and they eventually ended up in New York City. In another incident, a Philadelphia schooner bound for Virginia and Barbados was taken. On May 16, a Spanish privateer of ten guns and thirty-six men slipped into Lynnhaven Bay on the Eastern Shore of Chesapeake Bay and surprised a ship carrying tobacco that was bound for London. Another ship, under Captain Cobb, fled before Spanish privateers going up the James River where he beat them off. On June 21, Captain Bartholomew Radford fought off two Spanish privateers as he entered Delaware Bay. In July, Spanish privateers set seventy British prisoners who were taken as prizes ashore in Virginia.

Spanish privateering in the year 1720 turned into piracy. Not all Spanish privateers had letters of marque from the governors of St. Augustine or Havana. A brigantine with 140 men, commanded by the Spanish mulatto, Captain Nicolas de Conception, cruised the Virginia Capes and sailed into Chesapeake Bay. They took a Philadelphia sloop with bread and flour and made it into a sister ship. Another prize was taken and sent to St. Augustine. Meanwhile, the only guard ship in the vicinity, the HMS *Rye*, was helplessly laid up in the Elizabeth River to be careened. When the *Rye* finally retaliated against the brigantine, it was able to win only one prize back.

Noting the wide latitude given guarda costas in Havana, it is not surprising that in June 1724, the guarda costa *St. Francis de la Vega*, which should have patrolled only the Cuban coast, was outfitted and commissioned by the governor of Cuba to cruise far to the north around the Virginia Capes. Commanded by Don Benito with a crew of Spaniards, French, Irish and English, it avoided the British guard ship *Enterprise*. The *St. Francis* took a slaver with 175 aboard, keeping 76 slaves as booty. Don Benito's crew continued to collect prizes, and they escaped the *Enterprise* with three ships, although the British were able to take back one.

Port Royal was still a target for Spanish privateers. In 1710, the city of Beaufort was established, renewing the settlement begun by Cardross. The new settlers had difficulties with Indians, Spaniards and the French. They also had to contend with the pirates like Stede Bonnet who infested the coast, hurricanes and epidemics of small pox and yellow fever, which took hundreds of lives. By 1723 and 1732, forts had been built to protect Port Royal Island, and the forts became the base for the two scout boats that comprised Beaufort's navy.

In May 1720, the Royal Navy had sent a ship, the *Flamborough*, under Captain John Hildesley, to clear Charles Town's coast of Spaniards and to secure trade. However, while the vessel was careened and supplied for a year's time, it had remained in the port, failing to cruise against the Spanish. William Rhett, renowned for protecting Charles Town in 1706 and taking Stede Bonnet in 1718, complained to the navy board that he had loaned Hildesley £1,000 to provide necessities for the ship and had yet to receive a penny for the debt. On top of this, Hildesley had hired out much of the crew to work in the area and was collecting a profit from their labor when he should have been scouting the coast. In this case, Royal Navy support was not all that it should have been.

South Carolina also had its own problems, dealing with both possible slave uprisings and Indian depredations by the Yamasee. Both groups found refuge around St. Augustine, which led to the impression that St. Augustine was continuing a full-scale war against Charles Town and its dependencies. In 1728, rather than face the Spanish on the coast, South Carolina forces led by Colonel John Palmer retaliated against the refugees in St. Augustine's suburbs. His force of three hundred Carolinians and one hundred Indians was meant to punish the Yamasee Indians and runaway black slaves. The invaders invested their settlements around the presidio and desecrated the mission of Nombre de Dios. However, with their goal fulfilled and lacking the ability to conduct a siege, they made no effort to take the Castillo and town. While St. Augustine remained safely in Spanish hands, the garrison failed to leave the Castillo and protect their Indian and black allies.

Much of the privateering condoned by Governor Benavides in the 1720s was technically illegal; war against Spain had ceased in 1720. So, too, was the licensing of guarda costas from Havana to sail beyond coastal waters. This did not stop the governors of Florida and Havana from offering letters of marque to commercial captains, who carried on a secret war against the South Carolina coast and Chesapeake Bay. Virginia governor Alexander Spotswood led the British effort to stop the Spanish privateers, identifying St. Augustine as their base.

Chapter Nine
New York's Pirates and Providers

The success of Woodes Rogers, Colonel William Rhett in South Carolina, Governor Spotswood in Virginia and Spanish authorities against pirates had put an end to their period of prosperity, so that from now on, it would singularly be a time of more open trade, protected by privateers.

While St. Augustine remained a Spanish stronghold, fending off the British incursion, it also began to trade in earnest with Charles Town and New York City. Trading and prisoner exchanges with the two cities allowed Spaniards to become familiar with these British ports. Charles Town had actually been trading with St. Augustine during the War of the Spanish Succession and only stopped when the Spaniards attempted to invade the city.

Ships from Charles Town and New York were lured to St. Augustine because merchants could obtain precious silver in exchange for food. St. Augustine also modestly exported oranges between 1713 and 1739 to both ports. While Charles Town continued to trade with St. Augustine in the 1730s, its merchants gradually dropped out, as it was regarded as trade with a potential enemy. As the War of Jenkins's Ear approached, the field was left to New York, a very profit-oriented merchant community that was detached by distance from the conflict in the Southeast. New York merchant efforts to trade with St. Augustine continued regardless of the fact that Spain and Britain were at war.

From St. Augustine's perspective, the chief motive for both this trade and privateering was the fact that the presidio was far from self-sufficient, and the city needed to import or seize goods to sustain its population, which would reach close to three thousand by the middle of the century. As noted, the voyages of the situado from Vera Cruz or the Royal Company of Havana were easily interrupted, and it was normally late—sometimes as much as two years—leaving St. Augustine to survive on its own. Furthermore, as the eighteenth century progressed, Spain broke down its traditional monopolies and allowed British merchants to support St. Augustine.

NEW YORK'S REPUTATION FOR PIRATES AND PRIVATEERING

During the colonial wars, New York was seen as a place friendly toward pirates and privateers. Beginning in the 1690s, enterprising New York merchants underwrote privateering expeditions. William Livingston, a Scottish immigrant on the rise, put together £6,000 to support Captain William Kidd's supposed mission to rid Madagascar of pirates. Merchant Jacob Blydenburg supplied Kidd's mariners with shirts, waistcoats, shoes, stockings, rum and hats and in exchange received part of the treasure Kidd took.

Such business was needed because, in the 1690s, King William's War had cut trade with France and caused New York's economy to collapse. Only two sectors of the city's economy flourished, and they both concerned pirates. The first involved pirates and privateers coming to New York to refit and reprovision their ships. Merchants sold them provisions and bought their loot, sending it on to European ports that specialized in luxury goods. The second involved merchant investment in expeditions, which went to the distant places the pirates gathered, where merchants could offer their services.

Easy access to New York harbor, the number of accessible hiding-places beyond its port and the laxity of its newly organized English government, made it a great rendezvous for pirates, where they might dispose of their booty and plan new depredations. Sailors roamed its streets, squandering their prize-money in taverns by drinking, gambling, carousing and carrying on midnight brawls and revelry. Captain Robert Kidd was not part of this, for he lived respectably in New York with his wife and two daughters. He gave piracy a good name since so many benefited financially from it.

NEW YORK'S GOVERNORS SUPPORT PIRATES

Piracy thrived in New York City from 1692 to 1698, due to the support of the governor, Benjamin Fletcher, who was the center of a network of corrupt officials. Governor Fletcher allowed pirates to enter New York harbors without fear of arrest, dispose of their treasure and refit. Merchants offered them credit and news about weather and sailings. Pirate ships were charged a fee per man to anchor in the harbor, after which their goods were delivered without any problems from the customs department. Once ashore, any one of them could openly buy gunpowder, food, supplies and alcohol.

Fletcher would inform London that he was working to get rid of piracy, while he was entertaining pirates like Thomas Tew in his residence. After his return from his first pirate voyage in 1694, Tew had become friends with Fletcher. Tew was respectably married and had two daughters, both of whom enjoyed the New York social scene.

Tew was born in Newport, Rhode Island and about 1690, he went to Bermuda. Two years later, he obtained a letter of marque from the governor of Bermuda, and local merchants provided him with a vessel, the sloop *Amity*, armed with eight guns and crewed by forty-six officers and men. Thus equipped, he set sail in December, ostensibly to serve as a privateer against the French in Gambia. But just out of Bermuda, Tew announced his intention to become a pirate, asking the crew for their support since he could not carry out his scheme without their consent. Tew's crew supported him, and they proceeded to elect a quartermaster, a common practice to balance the captain's power.

In late 1693, Tew's ship reached the Red Sea and successfully took an Ottoman ship with a fortune in booty. When he returned to New York, he scrupulously paid off his Bermuda backers, who gained fourteen times the value of the vessel. In November 1694, Tew's career again crossed Fletcher's as the pirate received a new letter of marque from the New York governor and set out for another cruise headed toward Madagascar. In September 1695, at the mouth of the Red Sea, a twenty-five-ship Mughal convoy slipped past the pirates during the night, but Tew and his compatriots pursued and took it. He was killed in the battle, thus ending his usefulness to New York's governor and to the city's merchants.

Most famous of all New York's privateers was Captain Robert Kidd, who only verged on piracy, but became a victim of his political enemies and was hanged as a pirate. He attempted to appear as a respectable privateer, even as he slipped into piracy. A Scotsman, Kidd arrived in New York in 1691, and he married Sarah Oort, twice a widow and one of the wealthiest women in the city. He had previously commanded a privateer in the West Indies, fighting French ships from a base at the island of Nevis, where he acquired the reputation of being a brave and experienced seaman. The infamous

New York's Pirates and Providers

Captain Kidd in New York Harbor Welcoming a Young Woman on Board His Ship by Jean Leon Gerome Feeris. *Courtesy Library of Congress.*

Governor Fletcher dispatched him to "privateer" off the New York coast. He was commissioned in 1695 by King William III to hunt down Thomas Tew, another friend of Fletcher's, as well as other pirates. Unknown to the parties concerned, Tew was already dead when the commission was issued.

Kidd had traded with pirates, knew where they gathered and was often planning voyages. He was recommended by Lord Bellamont, governor of Barbados at the time, to the British government as a person fit to be entrusted to command a government ship to cruise against pirates. He, however, was not offered a position. In 1695, Lord Bellamont and others who had known Kidd in Barbados were anxious to share in the wealth he had obtained from privateering. Robert Livingston of New York organized the Bellamont investors among England's lords to support Kidd's pirate hunting expedition to the Indian Ocean. Kidd went to England to obtain further support, and the investors fitted out a ship at their own expense and gave its command to Kidd. He sailed out of London and then Plymouth in May 1696 in the *Adventure Galley*, a hybrid with oars for coastal marauding, thirty guns and seventy crewmen. However, he needed his crew to be twice as large in order to board the enemy, and he went first to recruit and see his family in New York. In the voyage across the Atlantic, he took a French prize, but this was no act of piracy—for now he had a privateer's commission to that purpose.

Watercolor of the *Charles Galley*, an English ship similar to Kidd's *Adventure Galley*. Painting by Captain Jeremy Roch, circa 1690. *Courtesy the National Maritime Museum, Greenwich, Connecticut.*

When he arrived at New York, he put up broadsides to attach more sailors. His terms were that every man should have a share of what was taken, reserving forty shares for the investors and for himself. He soon increased his crew to 155 men. During the expedition to the Indian Ocean, he veered toward lucrative piracy. On his return in 1698, Bellamont, now the governor of New York and New England, received him in Boston. While he was the very man who had invested him, Bellamont now had orders from London to arrest Kidd, and he fulfilled them. Kidd and his crew were sent to England to be tried before Parliament. Though he received support from some of his investors and friends, he was hanged by the neck in 1701. This merchant of New York with powerful friends could not live down his acts of piracy.

WALTONS SUPPLY ST. AUGUSTINE

New York merchants were willing to not only invest in privateers like Kidd but also to supply presidios that were threats to the British Empire, even in times of peace. St. Augustine's presidio economy fit New York's interest because victualing troops had become the city's chief enterprise, facilitating British expeditions against French Canada. New York merchants had actually supplied St. Augustine as early as 1683, when Dutchman Philip Federico entered its harbor by chance in his sloop. Moreover, in the eighteenth century, Spain broke down its earlier rigid trade monopolies, and as Britain was often at peace with Spain from 1713 to 1739 and again in 1748 to 1762, trade possibilities existed. Both St. Augustine and New York City benefitted from the situation.

The key figure in the relationship was William Walton, New York's most successful merchant from the 1730s. Born in 1705, he married Cornelia Beekman twenty-seven years later, and both had their portrait done by John Wollaston as a sign of their exalted position. Walton built the city's largest mansion, became a member of the governor's council and was tied to other New York merchant families. He became an expert in supplying armies and fortresses. On June 9, 1746, clearance was given to his ship, *William & Mary*, to supply the captured French fortress of Louisbourg on Cape Breton Island, taken by a New England expedition in 1745.

Antonio de Benavides, the same St. Augustine governor who had issued letters of marque to encourage raiding of British colonies, signed a contract with William Walton in 1726 to supply St. Augustine. Philip V had given Florida governors the privilege of negotiating contracts for provisioning the garrison. Walton's agents and captains were now able to regularly visit St.

William Walton by John Wollaston, circa 1750. *Courtesy of the New-York Historical Society.*

Augustine. His ships would provide supplies in 1731 and from 1736 to 1739, under an agreement with Benavides's successor, Manuel Montiano. From 1734, other New York ships began to call at St. Augustine and from 1737 to 1739, no less than twenty New York ships called there, replacing Charles Town as the chief source of British trade. In March 1738, the New York sloop *Don Carlos* returned from St. Augustine with a cargo of candied fruit and vegetables and in October, another New York ship, the *Dom Philip*, returned from St. Augustine with three casks of oranges. In 1734, Walton had sent ten-year-old Jesse Fish to live with the Herrera family in St. Augustine, where he would learn Spanish and act as Walton's agent as he grew up.

However, war clouds made this trade precarious. In February 1737, the New York Council forbade the sale of provisions to Spaniards. To clarify this, the council specified on March 5, 1738, that sending supplies to St. Augustine was prohibited. But Walton did not desist and still fulfilled his obligations to St. Augustine, for he was making a tidy profit in the trade. It remained to be seen what would happen to Walton's St. Augustine connection when the War of Jenkins's Ear was declared in 1739, and war continued until 1748. After initial difficulties, a compromise was worked out between Governor Montiano and Walton. On May 27, 1747, with the war not yet over, the New York Council gave permission for Walton and his sons, William Jr. and Jacob, to carry Spanish prisoners to St. Augustine. Three days later, the New York sloop *Don Carlos* carried them to St. Augustine, smuggling supplies along as well.

A conflict developed between New York and St. Augustine authorities beyond the issue of supply. While not a plantation colony, New York was involved in the slave trade and about 10 percent of the colony's population were black slaves, more than any northern British colony. This situation led to conflict over the enslaving of Spanish citizens, something that had first become an issue in 1668 when Searles had tried treating all of St. Augustine's blacks as slaves. Many of St. Augustine's blacks were legally free, but when Spanish ships were captured by New York privateers during the War of Jenkins's Ear, the privateers attempted to profit by claiming the right to sell blacks as slaves. As early as 1739, before Britain had declared war on Spain, John Lush, captain of the twenty-gun sloop *Stephen and Elizabeth* had captured at least five Spanish vessels and a larger French ship flying Spanish colors in the Caribbean, so that he had over a hundred Spanish prisoners when he arrived in New York six months later. Among them were nineteen blacks and mulattos, whom he claimed were slaves; the admiralty court agreed, and they were sold to New York families. Five of the captives,

Ye Execution of Goff ye Neger of Mr. Cochins on ye Commons, undated. *From* Valentine's Manuel of the Corporation of the City of New York, *1860*.

led by Juan de la Silva, became implicated in the Great Negro Plot of 1741 but defended themselves so well as freemen that it was thought they obtained outside legal council. Only Silva was hanged.

Other "Spanish negros" who were treated as slaves in New York were accused of being of an important segment of the Great Negro Plot to destroy rich whites and cooperate with a Spanish and "popish" invasion of New York. In the aftermath of the revolt, the New York courts found the Spanish negros an easy scapegoat and sentenced several to be hanged or burned at the stake. Such a violation of the rights of Spanish prisoners of war became know in St. Augustine, and Governor Montiano protested and looked for friends on the governor's council like William Walton. Walton was sympathetic, for he had defended his slaves from being accused of participation in the plot, and he was not a slave trader. Still, the courts refused to consider the Spanish negros to be free. From 1746 to 1747, New York merchants and privateers continued to capture blacks, morenos and pardos and sell them in New York as slaves. The freemen retorted that they were "free subjects of the King of Spain."

In August 1748, a British privateer under Captain Robert Troup seized a privateer from Havana, the *Nuestra Señora del Carmen*, and its forty-five black crew members. Technically, the action took place after peace had been signed, so the crew should have been freed. However, in the New York admiralty court, the blacks were again treated like slaves. Despite rebuffs by New York authorities, Montiano's successor, Melchor Navarrete, continued the effort into the 1750s to have these blacks freed, claiming that no Spaniard would allow slaves to serve on a privateer for fear of losing them and that free men of color were numerous in the Spanish Empire. He felt the New York policy of treating them as slaves was meant to terrorize free blacks so that they would not serve on Spanish privateers. After four years of protest, New York governor George Clinton did release two of the original forty-five blacks, a mere token of recognition of the free status of blacks in the Spanish colonies.

After the war, Walton family ships were again bringing foodstuffs to St. Augustine, under agreement with the Royal Company of Havana. In 1754 and 1755, trade was brisk enough for William Walton's grandson to write about an "Act of Cash received by William Walton from Jesse Fish, [a] New York-born agent of [his] in St. Augustine to defray expenses at St. Augustine and Havana on the said company business." Thus, the illicit trade of New York merchants like the Waltons continued to sustain St. Augustine.

In New York, commerce with the opportunity to profit always dominated politics. Pirate and privateering activities were investments created by the governors and merchants. It became known for its clandestine trade and welcomed pirates. However, New York privateers raided Spanish ships and attempted to sell the free black crew members as slaves. This policy was continually denounced by the governors of St. Augustine, through their connections with New York's merchants. In fact, under various contracts, the Walton merchant family provided New York's famous flour to feed St. Augustine from 1726 to the 1750s, in spite of the fact that Britain and Spain were often at war.

Chapter Ten
The Second Privateer War

The War of Jenkins's Ear and its continuation with the War of Austrian Succession kept Britain and Spain hostile from 1739 to 1748. British merchants and bankers had demanded access to Spanish markets, and Spanish colonists found British manufactures desirable, so that smuggling was widespread. Under the 1729 Treaty of Seville, the British had agreed not to trade with the Spanish colonies except under extreme conditions and restricted that trade to a single annual ship under the asiento slave trade monopoly. As noted, the terms also permitted the Spanish to board British vessels in Spanish waters. In 1731, a Spanish guarda costa off the coast of Havana boarded the English privateer *Rebecca* as its captain, Robert Jenkins, was making his way from Jamaica to London. The Spanish authorities were unable to find evidence of misdoings but, in the process, they tortured Jenkins, and the guarda costa's captain, Juan Fandino, finally sliced off Jenkins's ear with his cutlass and challenged him to take it to King George. Jenkins did just that, exhibiting his pickled ear at Parliament. This heightened the war fever against Spain, a fever that was driven by the British desire for commercial and military domination of the Atlantic. Prime Minister Robert Walpole reluctantly declared war on Spain on October 23, 1739. Privateers were now needed by both sides, and most pirates were more than willing to serve in that capacity.

The Stono Rebellion

Britain's declaration of war on Spain coincided with the great Stono slave uprising in South Carolina, which broke out at a store on the Stono River, midway between Charles Town and Port Royal. It was the focus of a bloody one-day black rebellion that was easily quelled by whites.

South Carolina authorities implicated St. Augustine in the Stono Rebellion. It had been the destination of the Stono blacks because of its reputation for freedom. As a result of Stono, South Carolina's Governor William Bull was ordered to issue letters of marque "to go cruizing on the Spaniards." He was urged to by Charles Town merchants like Robert Pringle, who hoped South Carolina's government would develop methods for seizing St. Augustine, "which [has] now become a great detriment to this province" because of their protection of runaways.

With hindsight, an official report in 1741 argued, "The Negros would not have made an insurrection had they not depended on St. Augustine for a place of reception...and that the Spaniards had a hand in prompting them to this particular action." It went on to say that Captain Sebastián Sánchez had come to Charles Town from St. Augustine in a launch with upwards of thirty men before the uprising and pretended that he wanted to deliver a letter to Georgia's governor, James Oglethorpe, who he knew very well was elsewhere at Fort Frederica. On his return, the St. Augustine captain reputedly visited every inlet on the Atlantic coast. It was feared by the South Carolina authorities that the slaves in St. Augustine would be guaranteed their freedom and that South Carolina was to be governed by the blacks as a dependency of Spain.

Privateers for Supply

With war realized and blacks in rebellion in South Carolina, Britain focused on Havana and, indirectly, St. Augustine. Havana gave Spain an advantage because it was a crucial link in Caribbean trade, with the superior facilities of its Royal Ship Yard, for no fleet could remain in the Caribbean for any length of time without seeking a port. However, the British also assumed that Havana was too well protected by its fortifications to be taken. It would remain in Spanish hands.

In 1738, Governor Montiano received a windfall of support from Havana, when an expedition against Georgia was pulled back for diplomatic reasons.

Along with military engineers, a master bricklayer, stone masons and iron cannon, he received funds for four craft to patrol St. Augustine's harbor. Two years later, Montiano asked the governor of Cuba for galleys, which arrived in April. Each had twenty oars, with swivels and a nine-pounder in the bow, and each was manned by thirty sailors and two officers. Three of the six galleys were commanded by Juan Fandino, the man who had cut off Jenkins's ear. Montiano also informed his superiors in Cuba that he intended to arm ships as privateers to supply food to the presidio. Using St. Augustine as their base of operations, Spanish privateers from Cuba and New Spain received letters of marque from Montiano, who encouraged them to prey on British ships from Georgia to Delaware Bay. It was a wise decision, for the situado would not arrive in 1739, 1740, 1741 or 1745. As mentioned, privateering for food was necessary to ensure St. Augustine's survival.

At the same time, Francisco Menéndez, a former Mandingo slave, served aboard several privateers and would serve on a privateer for the rest of the war, hoping his reputation might get him a post in Havana and, from there, a post in Spain. Originally a black slave from South Carolina,

Reconstruction of the Second Fort Mose. Drawing based on research by Albert Manucy and Luis Arana. *Courtesy Florida Museum of Natural History.*

he had escaped to St. Augustine, where he was granted his freedom as a subject to the king of Spain. He had been a free black military leader, serving as a commander of the pardo and moreno militia at Gracia Real de Santa Teresa de Mose since 1726. Menéndez led several raids on South Carolina from this fort.

In May 1740, General James Oglethorpe's army marched into Florida, initially overrunning Fort Mose; days later, however, Spanish troops and Fort Mose militia drove the British out, destroying the fort in the process. The loss of the troops at Fort Mose made it difficult for Oglethorpe to continue his siege. Under the Castillo's guns, Fandino's galleys tried to cut off Oglethorpe's artillery on Anastasia Island from the rest of his army. The siege ended when oared galliots arrived from Havana with supplies. They landed at Matanzas as pirates had done in the past and, using oared vessels, moved up the river. After a brief conflict, they found that Oglethorpe had left, which opened up the path to St. Augustine. Fortifications to protect the Matanzas Inlet would be completed two years later, so that it would no longer be open to an enemy.

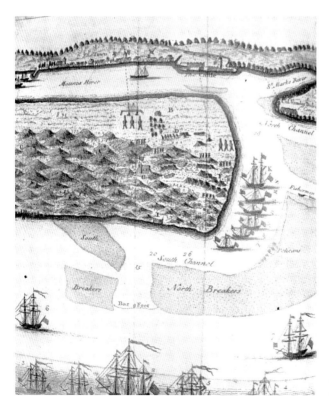

Map of Oglethorpe's siege of St. Augustine by Thomas Silver, 1740. *Courtesy of Yonge Library of University of Florida.*

The Second Privateer War

It was then that St. Augustine's privateer war against the British colonies began in earnest. At the end of the year, Governor Montiano armed a sloop, the *Campechana*, and gave it to Joseph Sánchez, who used it to capture a ship with wheat. However, Sánchez decided to retire, and when Montiano looked about for a new captain, Fandino sought the ship. He took it to Charles Town, where he captured the pilot's launch and sent it to St. Augustine. South Carolina authorities thought the knowledgeable pilots would lead Spanish expeditions against Charles Town. This was followed by the capture of a British schooner filled with rice and flour. When he returned to St. Augustine in December, it was because of the cold weather. By the end of the year, forty British ships had been taken officially to prevent hunger in St. Augustine.

On May 26, 1741, Captain Pedro de Estrada brought in British vessels containing corn, pork, pitch and tar to St. Augustine. On June 15, a Cuban privateer commanded by Luis Silvério brought in a small British sloop carrying corn and flour.

Spanish privateer captains carried out more raids against Carolina in 1741. Sponsored by Montiano, Joseph Estrada, with Francisco Menéndez in support, made attacks on the North Carolina coast at Ocracoke and Brunswick. While at Brunswick, the raiders burned a warehouse and two ships under construction and sent ships carrying rice to St. Augustine. On his return, Captain Estrada took five British prizes carrying rice, paper, wood and glass. St. Augustine's admiralty court now did a lively business in prizes.

In June 1742, Montiano brought together a fleet from Havana with his own from St. Augustine for a total of fifty-one ships and 2,800 sailors and soldiers to attack the British post at Fort Frederica on St. Simons Island, Georgia. The new colony had no slaves, but it was felt that those in nearby South Carolina would stage an uprising as they had at Stono and join the Spanish. In Cuba problems had emerged, when its governor, Juan Francisco de Guemes, began organizing his fleet. He did not want to weaken Havana, which needed at least 4,000 men to defend it. He managed to raise only 600 regulars and 700 militia, chiefly pardos and morenos, as well as enough launches and half galleys to transport 500 men. This force, carrying instructions for Montiano, left Havana for St. Augustine, where it picked up Montiano's contingent. The combined fleet, however, took sixteen days to sail from St. Augustine to St. Simons Island due to bad weather.

The Spanish naval force was not as powerful as its numbers suggest because many of the best warships were mere galleys and half galleys, with evidently no ships-of-the-line. Oglethorpe's intelligence also claimed

Free black militia man, Havana, 1770–76.
Courtesy Archivo General de Indias, Seville.

that the troops from Havana and St. Augustine did not get along, having separate camps. After a defeat at Bloody Marsh on July 18, Montiano sent three galleys to explore the possibility of reaching Fort Frederica by the shallow coastal waters that surrounded the island under naval Lieutenant Adrian Cantein. However, this also failed, and Montiano decided to return to St. Augustine.

Elsewhere, Spanish privateers in Beaufort, South Carolina threatened the town's maritime activity. The Spanish privateers rendezvoused in the large natural harbor provided by Cape Lookout Harbor. Here, they could anchor in protected waters, careen their vessels, obtain water and wood from the surrounding area and maintain a constant watch for coastal vessels, especially those passing through Topsail Inlet. The Spanish presence brought about agitation in Beaufort for fortifications at Cape Lookout. From there, Spanish privateers raided the Beaufort area on three occasions between June and September 1747. It had been necessary to muster local troops to resist the intruders. The Spaniards took several vessels in Beaufort's harbor and in August, they put a landing party ashore and actually occupied the town.

A force of local militiamen was able to take Beaufort back, and the Spanish privateers left soon after, their ships filled with rice and flour.

Spanish privateers were also found around Bear Island, North Carolina. During the Spanish alarm of 1747, the island was invaded twice. The authorities decide to erect a fort there, but it is not clear if the orders were carried out.

Privateers from St. Augustine raided as far north as the Delaware Bay and River. In the 1740s, privateers aimed at taking the Delaware port of New Castle. On July 12, 1747, twenty French and Spanish sailors landed near New Castle and plundered the houses of James Hart or Edmond Liston. They came in the afternoon and captured a black girl, who was crabbing with Liston's daughter, and bound her and put her in a boat. They then attacked Liston's house, armed with guns, pistols and cutlasses, and took his money, three slaves and keys. They compelled Liston to lead them to Hart's nearby plantation. Hart bolted his doors, but they threatened to burn it down. The house was bombarded and, after Hart's wife was wounded, he opened the doors. The house was plundered and the booty, including his black slave, loaded onto a boat. The Delaware Council was informed, and measures for defense were discussed, but the Pennsylvania Assembly was not cooperative.

A year later, New Castle was again threatened by the arrival of a Spanish privateer brig of fourteen guns and 160 men. When the ship anchored about ten miles below New Castle to await a favorable tide, a British prisoner on board, George Proctor, swam ashore and warned New Castle. He noted that it was Captain Vincent Lopez's plan to capture a ship near New Castle and pillage the town. When the privateer appeared flying English colors as a ruse, the citizens gave it a warm welcome with cannon. Finding he had lost the element of surprise, Lopez decided to retreat and hoisted his Spanish colors.

When the war was over, Francisco Menéndez continued to sail the seas on a Spanish ship to raid British vessels. In 1751, he was captured by the British and tortured. Attempts to sell him into slavery failed and a year later, he was ransomed, returning to his home at St. Augustine. After his return he was asked to rebuild Fort Mose. The renewed black community remained until the British took control of Florida in 1763. Menéndez was evacuated with the Fort Mose community for resettlement in Cuba. There, he established a similar community called St. Augustine of the New Florida. He died where he hoped to live, in Havana.

New Castle's
Court House,
1732. *Author's
collection.*

BRITISH COLONIES REACT

The British governments struggled with the problem of protecting their coasts from the Spanish privateers. Delaware was a proprietary colony of the Penn family, consisting of three counties and sharing Pennsylvania's governor. The Pennsylvania Assembly, dominated by pacifist Quakers, sidestepped defense issues by claiming its authority went only to twelve miles above New Castle and that defense was the responsibility of Delaware's own assembly. Thus, Delaware was cut off from Pennsylvania's defense funding, and its only real source of protection was the Royal Navy.

The defense situation was also acute in South Carolina and Georgia. Spaniards and their Indian allies could penetrate the coastal waters with shallow-draft periaguas and silently approach unsuspecting settlements. By 1702, South Carolina had created scout corps to detect the approach

Engraving depicting a Timucan piroque by Jaques Le Moyne and Theodore De Bray, circa 1565. *Courtesy of St. Augustine Historical Society.*

of raids from St. Augustine. These scouts patrolled the coastal waters in periaguas made from cypress or cedar logs and acted as marines, prepared to fight on shore if necessary. The canoes were large enough to carry swivel guns and occasionally used a sail, although oars remained the chief means of propulsion. When the settlement of Georgia began in 1737, South Carolina loaned a scout boat under Captain William Ferguson to patrol the inland waters south of Savannah. Eventually, South Carolina decided to disband the scout boat, but Oglethorpe immediately took it on and used it as a prototype for several scout vessels to protect Georgia's coast.

In cooperation with South Carolina, Georgia also recruited captains and ships for a small defensive navy. David Braddock had been first mate on a rice ship captured by a Spanish privateer off the Carolina coast in 1740 and imprisoned in St. Augustine's Castillo. He escaped and made his way up the coast to Georgia where Oglethorpe placed him in command of a naval schooner. Braddock's vessel helped repel Montiano's invasion of Georgia in 1742. He was then hired by the State of South Carolina to command one of their two new half galleys to protect the colony at the southern tip of Hilton Head Island. In 1746, he moved to Savannah, where he received a large land grant for his services and became a member of the governor's council.

He commanded Georgia's scout boat and became a highly successful privateer against Spanish shipping. Because of his success as a captain of scout boats and privateers, he was elected to the Lower House of Assembly when Georgia changed from a trusteeship to a royal province in 1754 and would serve until his death in 1759.

St. Augustine came into its own as a privateer base during the War of Jenkins's Ear. It was supposedly the objective of the Stono uprising in 1739, and South Carolina authorities continued to be outraged by the city's policy of freeing slave refugees. St. Augustine's privateers not only struck the Carolina and Georgia coasts but also raided as far north as the Delaware River. Some of their privateers continued their forays after the war ended, slipping into piracy. Reacting to the Spanish incursions, South Carolina and Georgia created scouts to patrol the coastal waters in dugouts propelled by oars, but they could not watch every Spanish privateer.

Chapter Eleven
The Seven Years' War

T he Seven Years' War began in 1756, and France replaced Spain as the chief objective of British privateers because France was now regarded as an aggressive naval power. King Ferdinand VI kept the Spanish Empire at peace, and Spain did not enter the war on the side of France until 1762.

However, while technically neutral throughout much of the war, St. Augustine's governors allowed French ships to use its harbor to refit their vessels. By 1758, French privateers were bringing British prizes into its harbor on a weekly basis. When Spain finally entered the war, St. Augustine privateers like the *San Christoval* captured three English ships, providing foodstuffs for the city.

New York's Waltons were able to continue to supply St. Augustine. Despite the formal peace, an embargo on trade with Spanish colonies was established in 1757 in New York, and Spanish ships were taken. However, on February 21, a report was made to the New York Council by William Walton on the necessity of shipping provisions to feed the starving city of St. Augustine. He contended that none of the supplies would reach the French enemy. Finally, in October, the embargo was lifted and provisions were sent to St. Augustine.

It was difficult for the Waltons to continue to supply St. Augustine because in New York City, privateers again flourished. Major General George Monckton returned from conquering the French island of Martinique and became governor of New York in June 1762. His popularity was based on his investment in a privateer, the *General Monckton*, following the example of many New York merchants.

SEIZING HAVANA

Before Spain was officially involved in the Seven Years' War, British war leaders planned to take Havana. The Cuban city was a military stronghold with thirty-five thousand people and primarily traded in sugar, tobacco and hides. It was the home of numerous free blacks and mulattoes, who established a craft trade and also provided one fourth of its military forces. The future of Florida would also depend on the outcome of a British expedition and siege of Havana in 1762.

To defend Cuba, Governor Juan de Prado had been appointed commander-in-chief. On February 1761, Prado arrived at Havana and began fortifications to strengthen the city. In June, a flotilla of seven ships-of-the-line under the command of Admiral Gutierre de Hevia arrived at Havana. They transported two regular infantry battalions, totaling 1,100 men. With these reinforcements, the garrison of Havana now numbered 2,400 regulars, including four squadrons of dragoons and the traditional pardo and moreno militia; the fleet amounted to twelve ships of the line manned by 6,300 sailors, gunners and marines. In manpower, the navy was twice as large as the army.

With the objective of taking Havana, a British expedition under George Keppel, earl of Albemarle, left Portsmouth on March 6, 1762 crossing the Atlantic. By April 25, the expedition had reached the recently conquered island of Martinique, where it added over 8,000 men. With more reinforcements from the British colonies, the force would amount to 21 ships of the line, 24 lesser warships and 168 other vessels, including privateers carrying some 14,000 seamen and marines, as well as 12,826 regulars and volunteers. In this case, the seamen were slightly more numerous than the soldiers. By June 10, they had landed in Cuba, surrounded Havana and opened a siege.

In Havana, authorities hoped that the city could hold out until a relief force arrived or disease decimated the besieging British forces. Thus, the fleet was kept in the harbor, while its sailors, gunners and marines were sent to garrison the fortresses of El Morro and Punta, on opposite sides of the harbor entrance, placed under the command of naval officers. Most of the shot and powder of the fleet, as well as its best guns, were also transferred to these two fortresses. The entrance to the harbor was blocked, when a boom chain was placed across it and three older ships-of-the-line were sunk behind it. Meanwhile, regular troops were assigned to the city's defense.

El Moro fortress, Havana, initially built 1589. *Courtesy of Wikimedia Commons.*

The British Fleet Entering Havana on August 21, 1762 by Dominic Serres, 1775. *Courtesy of Wikimedia Commons.*

El Moro fortress became the focus of the siege as British artillery bombarded it, while the defenders sortied to offset the breaches in the walls. Yellow fever, heat and a lack of potable water rapidly took their toll on the British army. Reinforcements of British provincials from as far as New York, Rhode Island and Connecticut replaced those regiments wasted by disease and finally on July 30, El Moro was taken. The commander of the fortress, naval officer Captain Luis de Velasco, was wounded and died the next day. He had begun his career in the 1730s by chasing pirates in the Mediterranean. His spirited defense shows that Spanish naval officers were versatile enough to fight both on land and at sea. With newly constructed batteries, the British began to bombard the city from several heights, and negotiations for surrender commenced.

On August 12, the capitulation of Havana was signed, guaranteeing the protection of property and respect for the Catholic faith. In the next week, the British fleet and their troops entered the harbor victorious. Their occupation lasted less than eleven months. As a result of the Treaty of Paris in 1763, Havana was returned to Spain, and on July 6, Cuba's government was back in the city on behalf of the king of Spain.

St. Augustine Evacuated

The British siege and capture of Havana placed St. Augustine in dire straits, and yet it survived by privateering and illicit trade with New York City and Charles Town. Food was still an issue, as the community had only its own oysters, fish and oranges for sustenance. However, in exchange for the return of Havana to Spain, Florida had been given to Britain. Thus St. Augustine would cease to be a Spanish imperial city. British soldiers, administrators and gunners arrived in St. Augustine in July 1763.

Spanish residents had been given about six months to depart. The evacuation had begun in April. Families boarded schooners, sloops and brigantines with their trunks and furniture. For many, they were leaving the town of their birth, where several earlier generations and been born and lived. In December, six shiploads of residents departed for Cuba and Campeche. The Spanish brigantine *San Jose y Nuestra Señora del Rosario* left port in December with ninety passengers, the largest group to depart that month. The ships also carried away the guns that had protected Castillo. Finally, on January 21, 1764, the last of the 3,000 Spanish evacuees sailed away.

Map of St. Augustine (at the evacuation) by Juan Elixio de la Puente, 1764. *Author's collection.*

New York's Walton family was still involved in St. Augustine's business affairs. Since the Spanish population had to embark quickly, Walton's agent, Jesse Fish, conveniently took on their debts. In exchange for a token sum from the town's Spanish agent, Juan Elixio de la Puente, Fish took over the deeds for much of the property with the understanding that he would try to sell them to the British newcomers. John Gordon of Charles Town also purchased several properties. On account of these transactions, Fish would claim "that considerable sums of money were due to Messrs. Walton, and to me." He had grown up in St. Augustine and sailed the coast as master of Walton family sloops, including one providing the presidio with flour and meat from South Carolina. The Waltons would continue to hold investments in British St. Augustine.

Thus, St. Augustine did not participate extensively in the Seven Years' War. French privateers made it their base until Spain declared war on Britain in 1762, and St. Augustine privateers were again in the fray. However, St. Augustine's fortunes were tied to Havana, and months after the war began, the Cuban city was taken by the British, and St. Augustine's privateering activities were limited. To restore Havana to Spain, Florida was ceded to the British a year later, and St. Augustine's citizens were evacuated to begin anew in Cuba and Campeche.

Chapter Twelve
Where Did St. Augustine's Privateers Come From?

The treatment of black members of Spanish privateer crews illustrates the place of blacks and mixed bloods in Hispanic society. Colonial society was legally divided into three main groups: peninsulars of European origin and criollos (American-born Europeans); mestizos of mixed white and Indian blood and also groups of black blood; and then Indians and mestizos who adopted Indian culture. This last description shows why the hierarchy of castes was not rigid or based on physical characteristics as in the English colonies, but that it was determined by the norms of culture one adopted. Anyone who practiced European culture, even blacks and Indians, was treated as white. It was necessary in a colonial society where, by the eighteenth century, miscegenation was so extensive that it was impossible to define racial origin by physical characteristics. Besides, freeing slaves was easy, so that in most coastal areas of the Spanish Empire, free blacks outnumbered slaves. This was why black sailors on Spanish privateers were usually freemen.

The castes also failed to be enforced in times of military necessity. In a presidio like St. Augustine where military demands were constant, governors felt that criollo militia had to be expanded by pardos and morenos, who were more effective than criollo units. Through militia service, blacks increased their social status. The status of a militiaman or sailor was technically available to most of St. Augustine's male society, except those who lived as Indians.

While blacks existed among St. Augustine's sailors, peninsulars and criollos were also present. Spain's Bourbon dynasty would put a strong emphasis on

Where Did St. Augustine's Privateers Come From?

Above: Drawing of black slaves filling water barrels during a layover at a port. *Original by Christopher Weiditz, Trachtenbach. Facsimile edition produced by Theodor Hampe, 1927.*

Right: Drawing of sailor in loose clothing. *Original by Christopher Weiditz, Trachtenbach. Facsimile edition produced by Theodor Hampe, 1927.*

the Spanish navy, which had been neglected in the seventeenth century in favor of the army. Ships were improved by Admiral Antonio Gaztaneta's designs, but manning them proved more difficult. From 1730 to 1760, there were about 25,000 sailors on the navy registers. Spanish sailors came especially from Andalusia and Cantabria. They were pressed or convicted into service in wartime, but there were never enough. When they existed, the flotas took the lion's share. In 1731, a battalion of marines was raised at Vera Cruz to serve on the Windward flota. However, marine units were never created in St. Augustine.

St. Augustine

Around 1700, St. Augustine's garrison included fifteen to twenty-three naval sailors, as well as a pilot and customs official. The latter position had been established in the early 1600s and often included a staff of constables, but in practice, they were creatures of the governor, who subverted the crown's sporadic trade directives.

A number of less exalted sailors and soldiers came to St. Augustine as laborers, serving sentences for crimes committed in Cuba or Mexico. In 1603, when Lucas de Soto was appointed St. Augustine's first constable of the customs, he was, in fact, a Cuban deserter who had been sentenced to four years in Florida for trying to escape. A Portuguese sailor, Manuel Melo, who died at St. Augustine in 1743, had been in penal servitude on Havana's galleys. Penal servitude had a long tradition in the Spanish navy because most galley crews and shipyard construction workers had been made up of convicts sentenced to serve the crown. Construction and maintenance of the fortifications required ongoing labor. However, in St. Augustine, there was the danger that the original sentence would be forgotten, making convicts little more than slaves.

In St. Augustine, the garrison of regulars and the local militia were the two forms of military service, and the members of the two groups would serve as volunteers on privateering raids. Originally, the garrison had been limited to peninsulars, but there were never enough of them, so by the middle of the seventeenth century, Mexicans and Cubans filled some places. The typical migrant to St. Augustine to serve in the garrison was a single male who had come from a large urban center, probably among the surplus landless population of Seville, Cadiz, Granada, Malaga, Cordoba, Mexico City, Puebla or Havana. He was swept from the city streets by a press gang or taken from the prisons and conscripted to serve in the presidio. As St. Augustine grew, its own criollos came to fill many places in the garrison because it was one of the few ways of making a living in the city.

St. Augustine's privateers gained volunteers from among the garrison's seaman and gunners. A profile of them before 1752 shows that gunners stretched back in service to 1715, the oldest being fifty-eight years of age, while the youngest were two twenty-four year olds who began service in 1743 and 1750. They were almost evenly split between St. Augustine criollos and peninsulars, with one being from the fortress city of Cartagena de Indies. Some were skilled, one serving as a mason. The sailors were younger; one was only seventeen, and many of the others were in their twenties, with the oldest only being in their thirties. Like the gunners, they were about equally divided between St. Augustine criollos and peninsulars. Joseph Marin was a boatswain. Sebastián de Herrera was a caulker of vessels, a native of the great port of Cadiz. Two others were designated for roping and rigging.

The city's militia consisted of only the inhabitants, who probably did not have a uniform in contrast to the white and later blue coats of the regulars. They contributed to the Castillo's construction, gained places in the garrison

Drawing of caulker filling the joints between the planks with tarred oakum. *Original by Christopher Weiditz, Trachtenbach. Facsimile edition produced by Theodor Hampe, 1927.*

and needed volunteer duties to make extra money. While at first the militia was made up of criollos, we have seen that pardos and morenos soon had their own units. When Governor Joseph de Zúniga defended St. Augustine in 1702, he had a force which included forty-four white militia and fifty-seven pardos and morenos. In 1706, Governor Francisco de Córcoles provided a Cuban expedition with volunteers, thirty infantry and about fifty "Christian Indians." In 1740, Montiano's garrison consisted of over three hundred Cuban regulars on detached service in Florida, sixty-one white militia, forty-three pardos and morenos and fifty armed Indians. With less economic security and better military competence, colored militiamen were most likely to serve on the privateers. In the West Indies and in the Carolinas, a propensity existed for blacks, both enslaved and free, to become mariners. They were experts at handling craft in the coastal waters and found the possibilities of serving on ships as a route to attaining freedom. Many slaves were placed on ships by their masters under agreement that they would be freed when they retuned home.

In 1742, Juan Fandino's two-masted brig was taken by the British. They reported that Fandino's eighty plus crew from Havana and St. Augustine consisted of "Indians, mulattos and Negros." While these populations were the likely sources for the ships' volunteers, it should be remembered that, to the English, all of Spanish society had dark complexions. Indians should not be discounted as possible sailors; it was remarked that while government vessels were often deserted by their white and black crew members at ports of call, Indian and mestizo sailors usually returned to St. Augustine.

While privateer crews were not colorblind, they did set their own status, which on a Spanish ship could be favorable to blacks. Florida's governors were military men, and they recruited their crews on the basis of their strength and ability as fighting men, not on skin color. Thus, the protests in the 1740s by Florida's governors against the New York admiralty court and privateers for treating Spanish black crew members as slaves rather than freedman showed how valued black crewmen were by Spanish officers.

OUTFITTING PRIVATEERS

St. Augustine existed for a military, not a commercial purpose. Unlike Havana, Charles Town or New York, it had no merchant class to outfit privateers and carry on regular commerce. Its governors came the closest to having the resources of a merchant and needed privateers or at least

Where Did St. Augustine's Privateers Come From?

trade with a potential enemy to supply the community. They may have been forced to do this as a last resort, but it was a constant in St. Augustine's continual struggle for survival. Governor Juan de Ayala Escobar acted like a merchant when he smuggled food from Charles Town and sold it for exorbitant prices in his shop. He was unusual in that he was born in Cuba and had family connections there, which helped him in trading. However, his successor caught him, and he would languish and die in a Cuban prison, even though he was popular in St. Augustine because he had prevented starvation.

Besides the purchase of vessels from Havana or Vera Cruz, St. Augustine built many of the small craft necessary for supply, invasion of the enemy or contact with the rest of the Spanish Empire. The ability to cross the sandbar at the entrance to its harbor created a need for the shallow-drawing galliots, frigates, barges, pirogues and launches. St. Augustine's governors promoted shipbuilding in the city to meet this need. Menéndez Aviles had built small vessels there when its resources for such enterprises included pine, enduring cedar and palm timber. By the 1590s, the town had a wharf built of such wood. It became scarcer in the following centuries, which limited shipbuilding possibilities to the production of naval stores. In order to win appointment by the crown as governor of Florida, Benito Ruiz de Salazar Vallecilla, in 1666, was required to construct a galleon during his first year in office, a feat he was unable to accomplish. He never gained the position. In 1735, Governor Francisco Moral urged the production of pitch, tar, spars and masts for use in the Havana shipyard. It was left to his successor, Governor Montiano, in 1744, to propose that a ship outfitting and building enterprise be established at St. Augustine. He hoped to erect a tar and pitch factory to supply the ship builders of the Havana Company. Apalache was to be the source of the masts. He also wanted to establish a company in Florida similar to the Havana Company, but was met with delays. Finally, in 1756, governor Alonso Fernández de Heredia began the manufacture of barrels of tar and pitch, which were used by the Havana Company in their shipyards. Ferdinand VI encouraged such enterprise, and in 1757, the first shipment of tar and pitch arrived in Vera Cruz, which shocked the city considering Mexico had been the source of the situado for almost two centuries. By the time the details of relief from port taxes on its tar and pitch had been worked out, St. Augustine was in the process of being transferred to the British.

PRIVATEERING WITH CUBA

Of the privateering captains who carried letters of marque in the 1740s, a majority were Cubans, although some came from St. Augustine. Cubans included Juan de Alarcón, Luis Silvério and Juan Fandino, the man who had cut off Jenkins's ear. Black officers Nicholas de Conception and Francisco Menéndez, an escapee from South Carolina, were from St. Augustine.

Cuba was the chief source of the privateer ships and crews gathered in St. Augustine's harbor. Havana and Santiago de Cuba had merchants to underwrite and supply sailors and soldiers to act as marines. Santiago merchants organized the attack on the Bahamas in 1667 when Robert Searles was there, and in 1684, merchants from Havana put together the expedition under pirate Juan de Alarcón that led to the successful burning of Nassau. These two Cuban forces did not use St. Augustine, although the pirate community in the Bahamas sought revenge by attacking St. Augustine. A Cuban fleet raised Governor Moore's siege of St. Augustine in 1702. In 1703 and 1706, Cuban-based expeditions once again occupied the Bahamas in a new alliance with the French.

When Charles Town became the objective of Cuban-based privateers, they had to stop at St. Augustine and take on volunteers and add ships. In July 1686, privateer captain Alejandro Tomas de León sailed out of Havana to attack Charles Town. At St. Augustine, he took on 153 garrison troops, Indians and the new black militia. While the expedition failed because of the elements, St. Augustine's governors still hoped to destroy the Carolina settlement. During the War of the Spanish Succession, Governor Zúniga proposed that a combined Franco-Spanish expedition sail from St. Augustine to Charles Town to punish it for its incursions. Two years later, after plague in Havana nearly scuttled a foray against Charles Town, Captain Jacques Lefebvre sailed from Havana with five ships, carrying about 300 French soldiers and 200 Spanish volunteers. The fleet first made for St. Augustine, where Governor Córcoles provided volunteers. The combined fleet and army sailed from St. Augustine on August 31.

In 1720, during the first era of privateering from St. Augustine, three Havana privateers were fitted out to raid the British colonial coast. Four years later, a Spanish guarda costa, *St. Francis de la Vega*, was outfitted and commissioned as a privateer at Havana by the governor of Cuba to cruise around the Virginia Capes. They put in at St. Augustine. In 1748, privateering in Cuba continued even after the war had ended, as evidenced by the capture of *Nuestra Señora del Carmen* by a British privateer.

Where Did St. Augustine's Privateers Come From?

Overall, between the 1720s and 1740s, St. Augustine's privateers grew in terms of crews and ships. Privateer captains from Cuba used St. Augustine's harbor, and the garrison had a small number of positions for sailors and pilots. The governor maintained a handful of small ships to supply the colony and keep contact with Cuba. Sailors and gunners in the garrison were potential volunteers and also helped to maintain ships. St. Augustine's militia, especially its pardo and moreno units, were likely to volunteer for privateering forays. Slave and free blacks become mariners and found that serving on ships not only enhanced their social status but also offered possibilities of freedom. St. Augustine's governors hoped to make their city a naval store and shipbuilding port by 1735 and provide support to the great Havana Ship Yard. Such dreams were cut short by the Seven Years' War, but could not diminish St. Augustine's role as a privateer center.

Chapter Thirteen
Affirmations

Pirates are misunderstood because they were not nearly as cruel, rich or democratic as they are portrayed. Piracy and privateering were forms of warfare, used by colonial governors to enhance their limited resources, much like the development of special units and militia to participate in guerrilla warfare. Privateers inevitably gravitated toward piracy. In St. Augustine, Spaniards were not just the victims of pirates—they also struck back at their enemies using privateers. The situation evolved from the time of Menéndez de Aviles and Francis Drake in the late 1500s, through the pirate raids of the 1680s and to the era of St. Augustine's privateering in the 1720s and 1740s.

St. Augustine's role in the 1680s as pirate target was never intense because it was not a rich city and its trade was minimal. In fact, it was a graveyard for pirates: Searles's crew failed to capture the flimsy pre-Castillo fort; Bréhal's men never sacked the town; Grammont's ship went down soon after he was repulsed; and his compatriot, Brigualt, was executed in the city square. Even the successful Francis Drake found the place only by chance and must have been disappointed at the slender pickings.

In the 1720s and 1740s, Florida's governors, with the support of Cuban governors, were aggressive in opposing British efforts to destroy St. Augustine. It became a privateer base to carry on war against the British colonies as far north as Delaware. Privateer captains came chiefly from Cuba, but crews were drawn from the segments of St. Augustine's garrison and militia. Free blacks of all hues from Cuba and St. Augustine were in the crews and British observers claimed they were the majority. Their status on Spanish privateers contrasted to the role blacks had in British colonies, where slavery was predominant, even among blacks who were sailors. The integration of blacks into Spanish society as freemen was considered a threat to norms of the British community.

Overall, an Atlantic perspective of St. Augustine has been necessary because of the importance of pirates and privateers in the Bahamas, Carolina, Havana and New York City. These places were involved with St. Augustine, the presidio, even though it carried on minimal commercial trade.

Selected Bibliography

Primary

Blacker, Irwin, ed. *Hakluyt's Voyages: The Principal Navigations, Traffics & Discoveries of the English Nation*. New York: Viking Press, 1965.

Cathedral Records, St. Augustine Parish: Baptisms, Marriages, Burials. N.d. St. Augustine Historical Society, St. Augustine, FL.

Johnson, Captain Charles. *A General History of the Robberies and Murders of the Most Notorious Pirates, c. 1725*. New York: Carroll & Graf, 1999.

Manucy, Albert, ed. *The History of Castillo de San Marcos & Fort Matanzas*. Washington, D.C.: National Park Service, 1955.

Oldmixon, John. *The British Empire in America*. 1741. Reprint, New York: Augustus M. Kelley, 1969.

Smith, Mark, ed. *Stono: Documenting and Interpreting a Southern Slave Revolt*. Columbia: University of South Carolina Press, 2005.

Spotswood, Alexander. *The Official Letters of Alexander Spotswood, Lieutenant Governor of Virginia, 1710–1722*. Richmond: Virginia Historical Society, 1882.

Secondary

Arana, Luis Rafael. "Aid to St. Augustine after the Pirate Attack, 1668–1670." *El Escibano* 7, no. 3 (July 1970): 74–91.

Arana, Luis Rafael, and Albert Manucy, *The Building of Castillo de San Marcos*. Fort Washington, PA: Eastern National Park & Monument Association, 1977.

Arnade, Charles. *The Siege of St. Augustine in 1702*. Gainesville: University Press of Florida, 1959.

Burgess, Robert, and Carl Clausen. *Florida's Golden Galleons*. Stuart: Florida Classics Library, 1982.

Bushnell, Amy. *The King's Coffer: Proprietors of the Spanish Florida Treasury, 1565–1702*. Gainesville: University Press of Florida, 1981.

Corbett, Theodore. "Migration to a Spanish Imperial Frontier in the Seventeenth and Eighteenth Centuries: St. Augustine," *Hispanic American Historical Review*, 54 (August 1974): 415–30.

———. "Population Structure in Hispanic St. Augustine, 1629–1763," *Florida Historical Quarterly*, 54 (January 1976): 263–84.

———. "Women, Marriage and Miscegenation in America's Oldest City, St. Augustine." Paper presented at the Hispanic American Conference, Houston, TX, 1999.

Evans, Cerinda. *Some Notes On Shipbuilding and Shipping in Colonial Virginia*. Williamsburg: The Virginia 350th Anniversary Celebration Corporation, 1957.

González, Antonio García-Baquero. *Andalucia y la Carrea de Indias, 1492–1824*. Granada, Spain: University of Granada, 2002.

———. *Comercio y Burguesa mercantile en el Cádiz de la Carrera de Indias*. Chiclana de la Frontera, Spain: Diputacion provincial de Cadiz, 1991.

Harbron, John. *Trafalgar and the Spanish Navy*. Annapolis, MD: Naval Institute Press, 1988.

Harman, Joyce. *Trade and Privateering in Spanish Florida, 1732–1763*. St. Augustine, FL: St. Augustine Historical Society, 1969.

Hoffman, Paul. *Florida's Frontiers*. Bloomington: Indiana University Press, 2002.

Ivers, Larry. "Rangers, Scouts, and Tythingmen," in *Forty Years of Diversity, Essays on Colonial Georgia*. Edited by Harvey Jackson and Phinizy Spalding. Athens: University of Georgia Press, 1984. 152–62.

Kamen, Henry. *Spain in the Later Seventeenth Century, 1665–1700*. New York: Longman, 1980.

Landers, Jane. *Black Society in Spanish Florida*. Urbana: Illinois University Press, 1999.

Lyon, Eugene. "Aspects of Pedro Menéndez the Man." *El Escribano*, 24 (1987): 39–52.

Manucy, Albert. *Sixteenth-Century St. Augustine: The People and Their Homes*. Gainesville: University Press of Florida, 1997.

McNeill, John Robert. *Atlantic Empires of France and Spain, Louisbourg and Havana, 1700–1763.* Chapel Hill: University of North Carolina Press, 1985.

Pennell, C.R. *Bandits at Sea: A Pirate Reader.* New York: New York University Press, 2001.

Pérez-Mallaína, Pablo. *Spain's Men at Sea, Daily Life in the Indies Fleets in the Sixteenth Century.* Translated by Carla Rahn Phillips. Baltimore, MD: Johns Hopkins University Press, 1998.

Phillips, Carla Rahn. *Six Galleons for the King of Spain: Imperial Defense in the Early Seventeenth Century.* Baltimore, MD: Johns Hopkins University Press, 1986.

Rediker, Marcus. *Villains of All Nations: Atlantic Pirates in the Golden Age.* Boston: Beacon Press, 2004.

Ritchie, Robert. *Captain Kidd and the War Against the Pirates.* Cambridge, MA: Harvard University Press, 1986.

"The 17th Century" under "Corsairs and Pirates." Bertan Collection. 2007. bertan.gipuzkoakultura.net/es/5/ing/8.php – 39k

TePaske, John. *The Governorship of Spanish Florida, 1700–1763.* Durham, NC: Duke University Press, 1964.

Waterbury, Jean Parker, ed. *The Oldest City, St. Augustine: Saga of Survival.* St. Augustine, FL: St Augustine Historical Society, 1983.

———, ed. *Firestorm and Ashes: The Siege of 1702.* St. Augustine, FL: St. Augustine Historical Society, 2002.

Wood, Peter. *Black Majority: Negros in Colonial South Carolina.* New York: Knopf, 1974.

Woodward, Colin. *The Republic of Pirates.* Orlando: Harcourt, 2007.

Index

About the Author

Historian Theodore Corbett is author of publications on the colonial Americas and the Revolutionary War, including *No Turning Point: The Saratoga Campaign in Perspective* (2012); *Revolutionary New Castle: The Struggle for Independence* (2012); and *The Clash of Cultures on the Warpath of Nations: The Colonial Wars in the Hudson-Champlain Valley* (2002). He is currently working on a history of the Revolutionary War.

Theodore Corbett.

Visit us at
www.historypress.net